ASTRO

THE
DONNING COMPANY
PUBLISHERS

ASTRO
A Celebration of 50 Years

by
David Hussey, Chair
Roger Robison, Vice-chair
Martin Colman
David Larson
Gustavo Montana
Beth Bukata
with
Bill Beck
on behalf of the
ASTRO
History Committee

The Donning Company Publishers
184 Business Park Drive, Suite 206
Virginia Beach, VA 23462

Steve Mull, General Manager
Barbara B. Buchanan, Office Manager
Richard A. Horwege, Senior Editor
Lori Wiley, Graphic Designer
Derek Eley, Imaging Artist
Scott Rule, Director of Marketing
Tonya Hannink, Marketing Coordinator

Steve Mull, Project Director

Library of Congress Cataloging-in-Publication Data

ASTRO : a celebration of 50 years / by David Hussey ... [et al.] ; with Bill Beck on
behalf of the ASTRO History Committee.
                p. ; cm.
    Includes index.
    ISBN 978-1-57864-515-2 (hard cover : alk. paper)
1. American Society for Therapeutic Radiology and Oncology—History. 2. Cancer—
Radiotherapy—United States—Societies, etc.—History. 3. Radiotherapy—United
States—Societies, etc.—History. I. Hussey, David H. II. Beck, Bill. III. American
Society for Therapeutic Radiology and Oncology. History Committee.
    [DNLM: 1. American Society for Therapeutic Radiology and Oncology. 2.
Radiotherapy—history—United States. 3. Societies, Medical—history—United States.
4. History, 20th Century—United States. 5. History, 21st Century—United States. 6.
Radiology—history—United States. WN 1 A859 2008]
    RC271.R3A88 2008
    362.196'994—dc22

                    2008032653

Printed in the United States at Walsworth Publishing Company

CONTENTS

FOREWORD

Working Committee
David Hussey
Roger Robison
Gustavo Montana
David Larson
Martin Colman
Beth Bukata

Reviewing Committee
Bill Moss
Herman Suit
J. Frank Wilson
Luther Brady
Malcolm Bagshaw
Ronald Dorn
Ted Phillips
Richard Hoppe

History Committee
David Hussey, Chair
Roger Robison, Vice-chair
Jesse Aronowitz
Martin Colman
Ronald Dorn
Ismail Kazem
Robert Kwon
David Larson
Douglas Martin
Gustavo Montana
Edward Ordorica
Herman Suit
Nagalingam
   Suntharalingam
J. Frank Wilson
Susan Yom

*P*reparing this fiftieth anniversary history of ASTRO has been a labor of love for those of us who have been involved with the project. *ASTRO: A Celebration of Fifty Years* is a story that recounts not only the history of ASTRO, but also much of the history of radiation oncology over the last five decades.

When my mentor Howard Latourette passed away about ten years ago, his son, at the funeral, commented that his father was very fortunate in that his career spanned almost the entire history of radiation oncology as it was practiced then. As I worked on this project, I began to feel much the same way. It's amazing the changes that have occurred in our specialty over the last fifty years.

John W. Gardner once said that "History never looks like history as you are living through it." That was certainly the case for me before I started working on this book. I noticed some improvements in the technology, but I never really appreciated the monumental changes that were occurring in our field, or the leadership role that ASTRO has played in radiation oncology since its founding in 1958.

Of course, history is very much the perception of those who are reporting it, and it can be perceived from many vantage points. We had an advantage because the History Committee has been collecting oral histories on videotape and audiotape from many of our members who lived through this era. They were a tremendous resource for the history committee.

In addition to the interviews, the committee had many other sources of information to draw from—Board of Director's minutes, *ASTROnews* articles, program notes, etc. Nevertheless, the committee had to conduct many special interviews of members to get specific information about certain periods of the society's history.

Two subcommittees were established to assemble this information. The Working Committee was responsible for much of the day-to-day work, interacting with Bill Beck, the professional historian and writer who put it all together, and Beth Bukata, our ASTRO staff liaison. All of the chapters were read and edited first by the rest of the History Committee and then by the Reviewing Committee, most of whom were in a good position to evaluate the history of the society over the last twenty to thirty years because they held major leadership positions.

Bill Beck of Lakeside Writers' Group in Indianapolis was wonderful to work with and helped make a monumental task easy. His experience and insight were invaluable. And Beth Bukata at ASTRO did yeoman's work in keeping everything on track. The members of the History Committee can't thank her enough.

For myself, I feel fortunate in having been able to participate. It was a fun project that gave me an opportunity to view not only the history of our society, but also much of the history of our specialty over the last fifty years.

We sincerely thank all those who lent their recollections and photographs for this book. I hope that you enjoy reading the book as much as we enjoyed putting it all together.

David Hussey
Georgetown, Texas
June 22, 2008

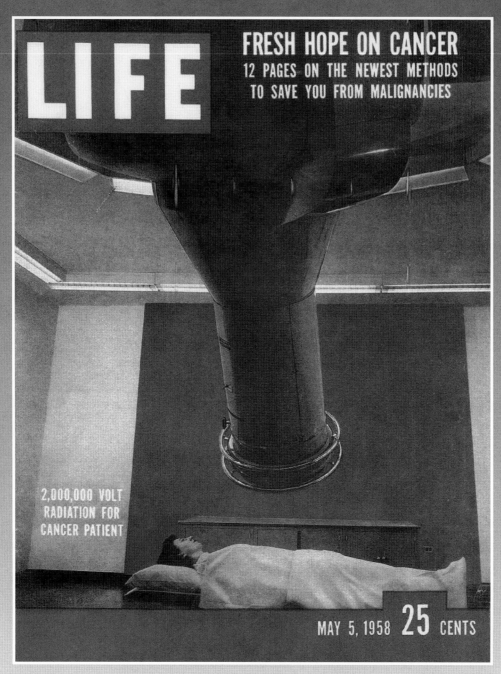

LIFE

FRESH HOPE ON CANCER
12 PAGES ON THE NEWEST METHODS
TO SAVE YOU FROM MALIGNANCIES

2,000,000 VOLT
RADIATION FOR
CANCER PATIENT

MAY 5, 1958 **25** CENTS

In 1958, the same year the American Club of Therapeutic Radiologists was founded, Life magazine printed this cover story on the promise of radiation therapy for treating cancer.

CHAPTER ONE

Radiation Therapy at the Dawn of ASTRO

The State of the Art in 1958

Radiation therapy was little more than a half-century old when the American Club of Therapeutic Radiologists was founded in 1958. The science of radiation therapy dated to the late nineteenth and early twentieth centuries. It traced its lineage to the discovery of X-rays by Wilhelm Roentgen at the University of Wurzburg in 1895. In Paris, Antoine Bacquerel discovered radioactivity in 1896, and Marie and Pierre Curie isolated polonium and then radium in 1898. Between 1896 and 1901, doctors in Europe first successfully applied X-rays and then radium to patients with skin cancers and carcinomas of the breast.[1]

Although it remains controversial, Emil Grubbe (1875–1960) is credited by some as being the first American to treat a patient with therapeutic radiation. The Chicago-based physics teacher and medical student claimed that he treated a carcinoma of the left breast of a Mrs. Rose Lee on January 28, 1896, ushering in the practice of radiotherapy in the United States.[2]

Others, including C. H. Brauer of David City, Nebraska; I. R. Kelly of Oakland, California; and Phillip Mill Jones in San Francisco, claimed to have used radiotherapy to treat cutaneous tuberculosis lesions at the turn of the twentieth century. In 1901, Francis Williams of Boston City Hospital published the first textbook of radiology, a 658-page volume that contained more than 63 pages on radiation therapy. As early as 1901, American physicians, including William Pusey, George Hopkins, and Clarence E. Skinner were using radiotherapy to treat Hodgkin's disease, ovarian cancer, cancer of the esophagus, and cervical cancer.[3] Other pioneers in radiation therapy included Eugene Caldwell and Mihran Kassabian.

During the 1920s and 1930s, Henri Coutard, Claudius Regaud, and Antoine Lacassagne at the Radium Institute of the University of Paris began to achieve cures of cancer of the larynx, pharynx, and cervix using radiation in place of surgery. They emphasized the importance of dose fractionation in the superior results they obtained.

By the mid-1920s, primarily in Europe, radiation as a therapeutic modality was being employed to fight tumors. Students from North and South America and Asia often went to Europe in the 1920s and 1930s to learn about radiation therapy as a medical specialty and returned to their host countries to develop it. Most radiation therapy specialists practicing in the United States in the 1940s and 1950s were not practicing it on a fulltime basis.

The Search for Megavoltage

What made radiotherapy more popular in 1958 was the increasingly sophisticated equipment that radiation therapists were able to draw upon for their practices. Working at General Electric in Schenectady, New York, W. D. Coolidge brought the gas-tube era to an end in 1913 with the invention of the hot cathode tube. Then, in 1922 he developed the first deep therapy tube of 200-kV.[4] A decade later, in 1932, radiation therapists were using X-ray generators operating at 600 to 800 kV. Megavoltage X-ray therapy was first achieved in Boston in 1937 with a Van de Graaf unit.

In rapid succession during the 1940s and 1950s, researchers in the United States, the United Kingdom, and Europe introduced cyclotrons, betatrons, cobalt machines, and linear accelerators. Nuclear reactors were able to create "artificial radium" isotopes such as cobalt, cesium, and iridium. Radar research during World War II led to microwave technology that was essential for the development of linear accelerators in the United Kingdom and United States. These powerful new megavoltage machines were capable of delivering radiation to deeply seated tumors.

In 1951, Ivan Smith of the Ontario Institute of Radiotherapy in London, Ontario, installed the Eldorado, later the Atomic Energy of Canada, Ltd. (AECL), cobalt-60 machine, which was quickly referred to as the "cobalt bomb," and began treating patients at the clinic on October 27, although it wasn't actually officially dedicated until mid-November 1951.[5]

Two years after the first cobalt-60 unit, the first linear accelerator was put into service in 1953 at the Hammersmith Hospital in London, England. In 1956, a linear accelerator was brought into clinical operation at Stanford University.

Also in October 1951, Harold Johns of the Physics Department of the University of Saskatchewan in Saskatoon unveiled the world's first noncommercial cobalt-60 therapy unit. Johns, working with graduate students and the local ACME machine shop, built his unit with literally no government assistance. He and his students at the university also developed a reliable and complete set of isodose tables for distribution to radiation therapists and other physicians.[6]

By 1958, the practitioners of radiation therapy were well aware of sophisticated new technologies that would allow US radiation therapists to make sophisticated advances in the years ahead. Most departments, however, relied on old-fashioned kilovoltage X-ray machines. There were very few betatrons or Van de Graafs in operation at the time, and many

Cobalt

By 1958, radiotherapy equipment evolution was moving to a new level of sophistication, bringing power and cost effectiveness that researchers had sought for more than a half-century. Orthovoltage and megavoltage machines were giving way to 1.2 mV cobalt teletherapy machines that promised to make radiotherapy a preferred treatment for cancer. Betatrons and electron were much sought-after machines because of their megavoltage photon, and prototype linear accelerators were just coming on the market in 1958.

"Cobalt absolutely flourished at the time," recalled Herbert Kerman, an early member of the American Club of Therapeutic Radiologists who worked on developing the first US commercial cobalt machines at Oak Ridge, Tennessee, in the early 1950s. "Cobalt really pushed the development of radiotherapy," Kerman said. "It was available, it was relatively cheap, and the maintenance was even cheaper. It became the workhorse of the practice. Cobalt just grew by leaps and bounds all over the country during the 1950s."[1]

Between 1939 and 1969, only 136 of the megavoltage X-ray therapy machines were sold. It would be the invention of the telecobalt machine in 1951 that first brought megavoltage therapy to community hospitals worldwide. From 1951 to 1961, 1,120 cobalt machines were sold, 422 in North America. In 1969, a 4-mV linac came on line that was cheaper and more reliable and began to capture some of the market served by cobalt machines. However, in 1986 there were still 2,400 cobalt machines in use worldwide, compared to 2,200 linacs. During ASTRO's first decade, the inexpensive and reliable telecobalt technology revolutionized the practice of radiation oncology.[2]

From 1948 to 1950, three different groups worked on the design for a 1,000-curie cobalt unit. British physicists J. S. Mitchell and Val Mayneord spent wartime service at the Canadian nuclear reactor, and they touted cobalt-60 as a practical substitute for radium and in telegamma machines. In 1948, physicist Harold Johns in Saskatoon, Saskatchewan, was listening. Also interested were the physicists D. Green and R. Errington at the Eldorado Mining/Radium Crown Corporation in Ottawa. In Houston, physicist L. G. Grimmett had been hired by Gilbert H. Fletcher at M. D. Anderson Cancer Hospital because of his telegamma experience. From 1948 to 1950 these three different groups worked on the design of a 1,000-curie cobalt telegamma machine. By 1950 all three groups were ready to have their cobalt-59 sources bombarded in a neutron flux (reactor). The MDA/GE project was under Oak Ridge control, and the sources were shipped to the Canadian reactor at Chalk River, Ontario, where they were inserted along with the sources from Johns and his independent group and from Eldorado in July 1950. The two Canadian sources were near 1,000 curies in July 1951 and were removed from the reactor and shipped to Saskatoon and to Eldorado/AECL in Ottawa for machine installation and calibration.

The MDA/GE source had a less favorable position in the neutron flux and would not achieve 876 curies until July 1952. Then, the Oak Ridge Institute for Nuclear Studies (ORINS) insisted on the Grimmett-designed General Electric unit being clinically tested in Tennessee for fourteen months before being sent to M. D. Anderson.[3]

R. Lee Clark, director at the University of Texas M. D. Anderson Cancer Center (left), meets with (left to right) Marshall Brucer, medical director at ORINS; L. G. Grimmett, M. D. Anderson physicist; an unknown ORINS official; and Gilbert H. Fletcher, chair of radiology at M.D. Anderson, to discuss a proposal by Fletcher and Grimmett to build a cobalt-60 unit for radiotherapy at the Houston hospital.

Herb Kerman was in the process of trying to establish a radiation oncology program at the University of Louisville in 1950 when he was approached by Marshall Brucer of the ORINS program to take a leave of absence for one year to go to Oak Ridge. That one-year leave stretched into two years, and Kerman worked with M. D. Anderson physicist Jasper Richardson to improve the shielding on the MD4 GE unit.

"We used a 200-curie source from Max Cutler at the Chicago Tumor Institute," Kerman explained. "By the time our 1,000-curie source was ready at Chalk River, Harold Johns and Sandy Watson had developed the first cobalt unit in Canada."[4]

It was February of 1954 before M. D. Anderson got to use its machine. In the meantime Eldorado became AECL and quickly dominated the market in cobalt machines. Johns sold his design to Picker, an American company, and they were able to capture about a third of the business. General Electric only made the one unit but other American manufacturers entered the field. The first American cobalt treatments were given at the Los Angeles Tumor Institute, which had secured 108 small pellets of cobalt-60 that were part of the clutter at Oak Ridge.[5] The 1,080 curies of cobalt were housed in a massive machine of local design that treated patients until 1962.

Other early cobalt machines were installed in 1952 and 1953 in New York City, Winnipeg, Chicago, Toronto, Philadelphia, and Albuquerque.[6]

By the late 1950s, a cobalt machine was a source of great pride for a community or university hospital. Robert Robbins, who headed the therapy section in the Radiology Department at Temple University Hospital in 1958, recalled, "by 1958, we had already acquired a small cobalt machine. There were no supervoltage machines around. Milton Friedman had a resonance transformer in 1958 at Memorial Hospital. A small hospital in Philadelphia got the first cobalt machine. We ascribed 'magical powers' to cobalt machines. The town went crazy for cobalt. Dick Chamberlain had a bottle of cobalt chloride salt on his desk so he could say that he had cobalt at Penn."[7]

Endnotes

1. Digitally Recorded Telephone Oral History Interview with Herbert Kerman, West Palm Beach, Florida, February 20, 2008, p. 4.

2. R. F. Robison, "The Race for Megavoltage," *Acta Oncol.* 34 (8), 1995, pp. 1055–74.

3. Notes, Roger Robison Personal Interview with Marshall Brucer, 1993, n.p.

4. Digitally recorded Telephone Oral History Interview with Herbert Kerman, Daytona Beach, Florida, February 20, 2008, p. 3.

5. E. R. N. Grigg, *The Trail of the Invisible Light*, (Springfield: C. C. Thomas, 1965), n.p.

6. R. F. Robison, "The Race for Megavoltage," *Acta Oncol.* 34 (8), 1995, pp. 1055–74.

7. Digitally Recorded Telephone Oral History Interview with Robert Robbins, San Francisco, California, November 11, 2007, p. 3.

radiation therapists were scurrying to get cobalt for their practices. There was only one linear accelerator in operation in the United States at that time, at Stanford University.

Radiotherapy in 1958

Most therapeutic radiologists in 1958 were educated in general radiology residency programs in the United States. General radiology programs were comprised of one year of training in radiation therapy and two years of training in diagnostic radiology. The knowledge base was much less developed in 1958. There were no journals specifically for radiation therapy. Additionally, the numbers of articles on radiation therapy per month in the English language journals of radiology were quite small, usually less than twenty.

A few of the general radiologists went on to receive additional training in straight radiotherapy, often in Europe. Only a limited number of physicians were trained exclusively in radiation therapy. There were very few institutions in the United States that trained physicians in this field, and even fewer were approved for resident training in straight radiotherapy. One such institution was the Penrose Cancer Hospital in Colorado Springs, Colorado.

Therapeutic radiologists in 1958 usually practiced in a hospital setting. There were almost no freestanding radiotherapy facilities in the United States at the time. Most of the treatments consisted of radiation therapy alone, or in some instances it was given preoperatively or postoperatively. The surgery employed to cure the patient was often radical in 1958, typically involving procedures such as a radical (Halsted) or super-radical mastectomy, Wertheim hysterectomy, radical prostatectomy, and amputations for tumors of the extremities. Organ sparing was not a concept that had yet caught on in 1958. There was little multidisciplinary therapy at the time and not many multidisciplinary clinics.

Brachytherapy was available—and had been since 1903–1904—because most departments had access to radium-226. Interstitial implants were performed with radium needles, or at some institutions with radon seeds. In many hospitals, the actual performance of the implant was by surgeons with the radiologists constrained to having the sources available and commenting on the dose and suggested duration of the implant. Radiologists had just begun to assume a more central role by the 1950s. The Ernst or Manchester applicators, or preloaded tandem and ovoids, were used for intracavitary applications. Afterloading techniques were just coming into use in 1958.

Herbert Kerman was building a regional integrated cancer center in Daytona Beach, Florida, in 1958. Kerman, who had trained at Duke and started his career at the University of Louisville, said that radiation therapy was "just coming into its own in the late 1950s. It was sort of blooming. What was developing was a specialty of its own. Most of the universities had combined programs. It was slowly beginning to separate into an identifiable specialty."[7]

Herbert Kerman, who obtained his American Board of Radiology certification in 1948, was named an ASTRO Fellow in 2007.

The Evolution of Radiation Therapy

In 1958, the year that ASTRO was formed as the American Club of Therapeutic Radiologists (ACTR), physicians who oversaw the delivery of radiation therapy treatments were called radiation therapists, or therapeutic radiologists. The term *radiation oncologists* had not yet been coined. The persons who actually delivered the treatments were called radiotherapy technologists; today they are referred to as radiation therapists.

Seymour Levitt recalled "many of the technicians were actually nurses who were trained to treat patients. Much of the radiation therapy was done part time by general radiologists, most of whom had one year or less of training, and many only three months or so."[8]

Marvin Lougheed, a pioneering radiation therapist in Montreal, Quebec, and an early member of ASTRO, took training that was not unusual for the society's early members. Lougheed entered specialty training in radiology in 1951 after a one-year rotating internship at the Montreal General Hospital, affiliated with McGill University, and one year of general practice. At the time, he was thirty-four years old.[9]

J. W. "Joe" McKay, head of the Department of Radiology at the Montreal General Hospital, made it possible for Lougheed to take a fellowship year in 1951–1952 at the Swedish Hospital's Tumor Institute in Seattle by providing the young doctor with a $5,000 stipend for the year. While in Seattle, Lougheed worked under Franz Buschke, one of the giants in radiation therapy in North America at the time.[10]

The Equipment in 1958

Although tremendous strides had been made in technology, the radiotherapy equipment used in 1958 was quite limited. Cobalt-60 teletherapy machines had only recently been introduced, and many radiotherapy departments were trying to acquire them.

Some of the larger academic departments had megavoltage machines, such as betatrons, GE Maxitrons with resonant transformers or Van de Graaff generators, but these were very uncommon. Most departments delivering radiotherapy treatments in 1958 relied on superficial, orthovoltage and kilovoltage X-ray equipment, except in departments that had a betatron, which produced high energy X-rays and electrons. Electron-beam therapy itself did not become popular in the United States until the 1960s with the increasing availability of betatrons and linear accelerators.

The only medical linear accelerator in the United States was developed at the Stanford University Palo Alto campus and installed at the Stanford Lane Hospital in San Francisco in 1956. This project was a collaborative effort between Ed Ginzton, a professor of high-energy physics, and Henry Kaplan, a professor of radiology. Kaplan recruited Joyce Lawson to be the first radiation therapy technologist on the linear accelerator.

Robert Robbins recalled that the Radiology Department at Temple "got a Van de Graaff machine in 1958 and a betatron in the early 1960s. We did simulations with a diagnostic machine, not a simulator. We got an IBM

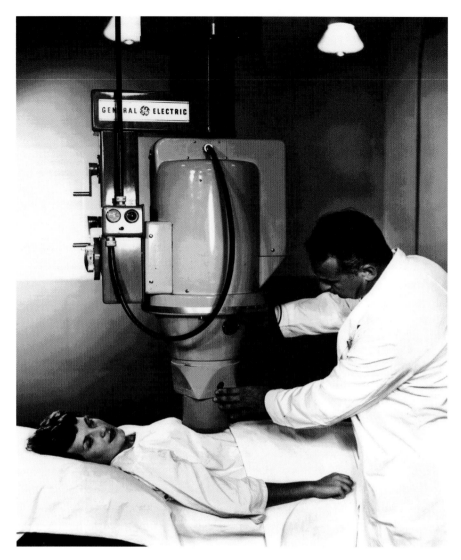

604 treatment-planning computer about 1960. We used to take contours of body parts and transfer them to paper and applied isodose curves to come up with a treatment plan."[11]

Herman Suit pointed out that there were some places with higher energy equipment. "There were already four and eight-mV linear accelerators in London and Manchester," Suit said. "Allis-Chalmers had 24 mV and higher energy betatrons in service. In 1957, while waiting for security clearance to start my two years duty with the U.S. Public Health Service, I had a one-month locum with a private clinic in Madison, Wisconsin, located within a block of the main campus of the University of Wisconsin. The equipment was a 24-mV Allis-Chalmers betatron. I was there as a solo physician, immediately after my training in Oxford where only orthovoltage equipment was available."[12]

There were no simulators in 1958, so patient treatments were set up using external landmarks, and the fields were checked with diagnostic X-ray equipment. There were no treatment planning computers, so the doses were calculated by hand, usually by the therapeutic radiologist. There

Carl M. Mansfield recalled the role of the physical exam in the practice of radiation therapy.

were relatively few physicists and dosimetrists working in radiotherapy departments in 1958.

Joseph Castro, who spent five years at M. D. Anderson Cancer Center in Houston, Texas, including training under Gilbert Fletcher and Herman Suit, attributed the emergence of modern radiotherapy to the development of technology. "I think it was what contributed so much in the development of radiotherapy," Castro said, "really bringing it into the modern era and convincing surgeons and internists and a whole host of other people that you actually could cure head and neck cancers, breast cancers and so forth."[13]

Carl Mansfield had trained under Simon Kramer, one of the early leaders of ASTR, at Jefferson Medical Center in Philadelphia in the mid-1950s. Mansfield said he has been astounded by the incredible change in the field of radiotherapy, especially in the area of technology. "When I started," he said, "even trying to determine the extent of the tumor was mostly by palpation, physical signs. That's a difference I notice, even nowadays. Many of the residents are totally unaware of a lot of the physical signs. Because CT or MRI or PET takes care of all those little clues. But we had to sort of work as detectives. You still have to do that, but not so much. There's a lot more information available."

The Stanford University Physics Department built this medical linear accelerator in 1956, utilizing a Varian Klystron and a Van de Graaf housing. The linac unit was installed at the Stanford Lane Hospital in San Francisco, California.

Relations with Referring Physicians

Most of the referrals to Radiotherapy Departments in 1958 came from surgeons or physicians in the surgical subspecialties, such as gynecologists, otolaryngologists, thoracic surgeons, urologists, internal medicine physicians (internists), and general practitioners. There were few medical oncologists in 1958, and those were usually in the special cancer centers. Radiation therapists typically didn't administer chemotherapy to patients. The internists or surgeons, who were the referring physicians, usually gave any chemotherapy which might have been given, at least what few drugs were available at that time.

The radiotherapy dose and technique was usually determined by the therapeutic radiologist, but not always. Occasionally, a surgeon would refer a patient and prescribe a dose, and even the field to be treated. This happened often enough that it was a source of consternation for the radiation therapists in 1958. Patient follow-up was another source of concern, because the referring physician often expected to be solely responsible for the follow-up care.

Nevertheless, 1958 was an exciting time to be in radiation oncology. The specialty was going through its formative stage at the time. What was missing in the practice was the existence of a journal and a society catering to the specific interests of America's growing radiotherapy community. Much of what was discovered by the pioneers of the specialty in 1958 formed the foundation for advances in the decades to come, including the establishment of the society that would ably represent the interests of radiation therapists for the next fifty years.

Endnotes

1. Luther W. Brady, et al., "Radiation Oncology: Contributions of the United States in the Last Years of the 20th Century," *Radiology,* 2001; 219: 1–5.

2. Nancy Knight and J. Frank Wilson, "The Early Years of Radiation Therapy," in *A History of the Radiological Sciences* (Reston, Virginia: Radiology Centennial Inc., 1996), p. 5.

3. Ibid., pp. 10–11.

4. Ibid., p. 2.

5. Ibid.

6. *Events in the History of the University of Saskatchewan,* "1951: Cobalt-60," http://scaa.usask.ca/gallery/uofs_events/articles/1951.php.

7. Digitally recorded Telephone Oral History Interview with Herbert Kerman, Daytona Beach, Florida, February 20, 2008, p. 3.

8. Seymour Levitt, *Questionnaire Regarding Therapeutic Radiology Practice in 1958,* 2007, p. 2.

9. Donna C. Lougheed MD FRCPC, "A Life in Radiation Therapy: A Personal Reminiscence of Marvin N. Lougheed MD FRCPC FACR," Unpublished paper, July 2007, p. 1.

10. Ibid.

11. Ibid., p. 3.

12. E-mail from Herman Suit to Roger F. Robison, January 9, 2008.

13. Dave Larson and Ted Phillips Tape-recorded Oral History Interview with Joseph Castro, October 22, 2002, p. 4.

The organizational meeting of the American Club of Therapeutic Radiologists at Barney's Market Club in 1955.
Left to right: Simeon Cantril, Bryan Redd, C. J. Ryan, Robert Robbins, Milford Schultz, Manuel Garcia,
Juan del Regato, Dale Trout, Milton Friedman, Donn G. Mosser, and Gilbert H. Fletcher.

CHAPTER TWO

Formalizing the Informality

A New Society for American Radiotherapists

There was perhaps no single event that motivated Juan del Regato to lay the groundwork for the establishment of a formal organization to represent the interests of American radiation therapists in 1958. A case can be made that del Regato was concerned about the paltry number of practicing radiotherapists in the United States, compared to Europe. He also was concerned about the lack of a professional organization structure to facilitate the future growth of radiation therapy in the United States.

The International Congress of Radiology was held in Copenhagen, Denmark, in 1953, and therapeutic radiologists attending the congress were invited by Jens Nielsen to participate in a special gathering of therapeutic radiologists at his department. The result of this gathering of radiation therapists was the formation of the International Club of Radiotherapists. Radiotherapists from the United States were eligible to join the International Club, but the United States was allowed only fifteen members. Del Regato, who was secretary of the North American chapter, and other delegates thought the United States should have a larger representation.[1] He also frequently expressed displeasure about the way existing national radiological societies in the United States had repeatedly refused to form a separate section for therapeutic radiologists.

At the time, most of the practicing radiotherapists in the United States maintained membership in existing radiological medical societies. These were the American College of Radiology (ACR), the American Radium Society (ARS), the American Roentgen Ray Society (ARRS), and the Radiological Society of North America (RSNA). American radiologists had been creating radiological societies since at least 1900 when the Roentgen Society of the United States (1900–02) was formed. It was renamed the American Roentgen Ray Society in 1902. Its membership came predominantly from the eastern states of New York, Pennsylvania, Ohio, and Massachusetts.

Logo of the Seventh International Congress of Radiology in Copenhagen, the site of the 1953 founding of the International Club of Radiotherapists.

The Western Roentgen Society (1915–20) was formed in Chicago in 1915, and it became the Radiological Society of North America in 1920.

The first multidisciplinary oncology society, the American Radium Society, was founded in 1916 with the support of a major radium company. The ARS, whose goal was to represent the interests of oncological surgeons and radium therapists, became the main membership choice for many American radiotherapists. Later, its membership included medical oncologists and nuclear medicine specialists. Although its membership was open to all eligible physicians, the ARS tended to attract academicians rather than private practitioners. This society required members to have published at least one paper.[2]

The American College of Radiology was founded in 1923 in California by radiotherapist Albert Soiland (1873–1946). In 1933, at the Chicago Century of Progress Exposition, the American Board of Radiology (ABR) was organized, and examination for certification started the next year. Requirements included one year of internship and three years of radiology residency/study. Certification could be in one of three fields, radiology, diagnosis, or therapy.[3]

Jens Nielsen, originator and founder of the International Club of Radiotherapists (ICR) and the ICR's first president from 1956 to 1959.

Above, left: Early logo of the Radiological Society, which became the Radiological Society of North America (RSNA) in 1920.

The RSNA Connection

Del Regato, a longtime member of the RSNA, began to invite fellow radiotherapists to get together at the annual ARS meeting in the spring and at the annual RSNA meetings in Chicago, which had usually been held just after Thanksgiving, in late November or early December.

The radiotherapists' meetings at the RSNA were more about fellowship, rather than business. Often, they were held in conjunction with the North American chapter of the International Club of Radiotherapists.

Luther Brady, who was then embarking on a successful career in radiotherapy at Hahnemann Hospital in Philadelphia, began attending the meetings at the Palmer House and various downtown Chicago steakhouses in the late 1950s. "The meetings of the American Club at the steakhouse in Chicago were very informal and mostly social," Brady recalled. "I went in 1957. Wherever ARS met and then at the RSNA, there were good friends, lots of fellowship and good food. There was not much business, and there was always a president elected for the meetings."[4]

One focus of the luncheon and dinner meetings that del Regato organized at both the ARS and RSNA was to define a practicing radiotherapist in the 1950s. Diagnostic radiologists still outnumbered radiation therapists by a substantial margin, and radiotherapists—particularly those in private practice—read X-rays at least a couple of days a week. Phil Rubin, who was then at the University of Rochester,

A group of charter members of the International Club of Radiotherapists pose for a 1953 photo in the garden of the Radium Center of Copenhagen. Left to right: Clifford Ash (Canada), Francois Baclesse (France), Elis Berven (Sweden), James Nickson (United States), Juan del Regato (United States), Simeon Cantril (United States), David Smithers (United Kingdom), Bertram Low-Beer (United States), and Bertis Evenius (Sweden).

remembered being urged by del Regato to attend one of the luncheon meetings because he limited his practice to radiotherapy.[5]

A complaint that del Regato heard from all of his colleagues in radiotherapy was that the other existing professional societies such as the RSNA and ARRS were hesitant to form separate sections dedicated to radiotherapy within the host society. While the ARS seemed to be an obvious membership choice for many American radiotherapists because of its focus on combating cancer, it too was not taking any steps to create a radiotherapy section. In later years, del Regato, Gilbert Fletcher, and numerous other ASTRO officers would serve as presidents of ARS.[6]

Another potential membership choice for the nation's radiotherapists was the RSNA. The Radiological Society of North America was perhaps the professional organization that radiotherapists felt most comfortable with joining because it concerned itself with radiology in all of its subspecialties. The RSNA's scientific program typically offered sessions dealing with the clinical, physics, and biology components of radiation therapy, and it encouraged the growing number of women who had served as radiology technicians to replace men who had gone off to the service in World War II to complete medical school to become radiologists in postwar America.[7] Early members Eleanor Montague and Norah Tapley had taken that route to a place of prominence in the radiation therapy community.

That wasn't the case with the American Roentgen Ray Society. Stung by criticism from radiotherapists about its limited coverage of radiotherapy issues, ARRS eventually came down on the side of diagnostic radiology and withdrew its support of therapeutic radiology topics at the organization's annual meetings and in the pages of its *American Journal of Roentgenology.*[8]

As time wore on, radiation oncologists were more likely to stay as members of the American Radium Society than continuing as members in the RSNA, primarily because the ARS remained an oncology society and dealt with the issues that radiation oncologists confronted every day.

A number of new radiology specialty societies were organized during the 1950s as well, including the Radiation Research Society in 1952, the Association of University Radiologists in 1953, the Society of Nuclear Medicine in 1956, and the American Association of Physicists in Medicine in 1959. Although the American Club of Therapeutic Radiologists was formed in 1958, most radiotherapists continued to have an affinity for the older societies as well.

"A Short and Friendly Discussion"

The initial meeting of what would become the American Club of Therapeutic Radiologists (ACTR) took place at Barney's Market Club in

Chicago in conjunction with RSNA's annual meeting at the Palmer House during the first week of December 1955.[9]

Del Regato called that first meeting for "a short and friendly discussion on the desirability of more of these gatherings."[10] Barney's was a three- or four-block walk from the Palmer House. Del Regato always called it "the steakhouse," never Barney's.[11] Verbal invitations were issued to a number of RSNA attendees, some of whom were the select fifteen members of the North American Chapter of the International Club of Radiotherapists. The six ICR attendees at that December 5 dinner were del Regato, Gilbert Fletcher, Simeon Cantril from Seattle, Milton Friedman from New York, Manuel Garcia from New Orleans, and Milford Schulz from Boston. Other US members of the International Club not in attendance at the dinner included James Carpender, Harold Jacox, Maurice Lenz, Ted Eberhard, Franz Buschke, Robert A. Caulk, and James Nickson.

Several friends and colleagues of the American ICR members also were in attendance, including Donn Mosser of Minneapolis, Bryan Redd of Atlanta, and Robert Robbins of Philadelphia. Guests included E. Dale Trout, General Electric's senior physicist and salesman at the Schenectady Works, and a C. J. Ryan, whose identity has been lost to history.[12]

A map of downtown Chicago showing the location of Barney's Market Club, the Palmer House, and McCormick Place (current location of the RSNA meeting).

The Chicago building that housed Barney's Market Club, as it appears in 2008.

The Best Steak in Town

Barney's Market Club

731 - 741 W. RANDOLPH STREET
CHICAGO

Famous For Food & Fun

A souvenir menu from the 1955 Barney's Market Club dinner preceding the founding of ACTR.

Those in attendance at that original 1955 meeting agreed that the chance to get together and discuss items of interest should be pursued. Del Regato volunteered to host a similar dinner at the 1956 RSNA annual meeting, a year later.

The Meeting at Barney's

On the night of December 5, 1955, Donn Mosser crossed Chicago's Loop to Randolph Street and checked his coat inside the door at Barney's Market Club to join a dozen other radiotherapists in one of the restaurant's paneled rooms for drinks, porterhouse steaks, and conversation. Mosser, a thirty-four-year-old Kansan, had recently returned to teach at the University of Minnesota after spending a year working and training with radiotherapists in Europe. The meetings of US radiotherapists held late each year in conjunction with the annual RSNA meeting would give Mosser and others in attendance a chance to catch up on the latest developments and to hear news of colleagues. In 1955, one-third of those who had dedicated their practice to radiation therapy in the United States were gathered in the back room at Barney's.

"At that time we attempted to identify all of the people practicing full-time radiotherapy in the US," Mosser explained, "and we figured that there were only about thirty-five of us in the country."[1]

Mosser, one of two surviving attendees of the 1955 meeting as the society approaches its fiftieth anniversary, recalled some of those at the Barney's meeting. "There was Jim Nickson at Memorial in New York City; Milford Schulz at Massachusetts General in Boston; Manuel Garcia in New Orleans; Simeon Cantril in Seattle; Justin Stein in Los Angeles; Walter Murphy at Buffalo General Hospital; and Milton Friedman who had a private practice on Fifth Avenue in New York," Mosser said.[2]

A large number of the physicians who exclusively practiced radiation therapy in the early 1950s were from foreign countries. Most American graduates were trained in general radiology programs that required only nine months of training in radiotherapy. Throughout the 1950s and even into the 1960s, most of those trained in straight therapy trained abroad.

Two of those who met at that 1955 meeting at Barney's in Chicago were among the triad of individuals who would later come to be responsible for many of the advances in American radiotherapy. Juan del Regato, who was then director of the Penrose Cancer Hospital in Colorado Springs, Colorado, had called the meeting at Barney's and presided over the gathering. Gilbert H. Fletcher, head of the Department of Radiology at M. D. Anderson Cancer Center in Houston, Texas, also was among the dozen attendees that December night and would help del Regato found the club, ASTRO's predecessor, three years later. The third member of the triad, Henry S. Kaplan, professor and chair of radiology at Stanford University, was not in attendance at Barney's.

Del Regato, Fletcher, and Kaplan helped mold the practice of modern American Radiotherapy and they were also founding members of the American Club of Therapeutic Radiologists in 1958. The American Club of Therapeutic Radiologists was the predecessor of ASTRO.

1956

Almost exactly one year later, on December 6, 1956, radiotherapists from North America enjoyed a "Dutch dinner" in a first-floor banquet room at the Palmer House in Chicago. From his office at Penrose Hospital in Colorado Springs, del Regato had sent invitations to all of the fifteen ICR members and other prominent radiotherapists well in advance of the meeting. This time, forty people attended, including thirteen of the fifteen members of the North American chapter of ICR. There was a strong delegation from California, headed by Henry S. Kaplan of Stanford and James T. Case from Santa Barbara. Morton Kligerman was there from New York City, and Isadore Lampe came down from Ann Arbor on the train.[13] E. Dale Trout, who had moved to Milwaukee to work for Allis Chalmers the year previous, was at his second successive meeting.

The Penrose Tumor Clinic in Colorado Springs, Colorado, in 1949.

The gathering at the Palmer House immediately asked Jim Case to chair the meeting. Case, a son-in-law of John H. Kellogg, a former staff physician at the Battle Creek Sanitarium, had been a president of the ARS and an RSNA Gold Medal recipient. He presided over what del Regato described as a "considerable and lively discussion."[14]

Bill Moss, who had trained under del Regato at Ellis Fischel State Cancer Center in Columbia, Missouri, in 1945, started attending the meetings in 1956. He was director of radiation oncology at Northwestern University in Chicago. He recalled discussing the concept of an organization for radiotherapists with del Regato when he was a resident right after World War II.

"When I was training under del Regato, he was talking about the club, which was his idea," Moss said. "He told me he called it a club in order not to intimidate the people running the RSNA. He didn't want it called a society."[15]

Case steered the Palmer House meeting in the direction del Regato wanted. When Franz Buschke, Jim Nickson, Donn Mosser, Manuel Garcia, and others suggested that future meetings include some scientific interchange, the radiotherapists agreed unanimously. J. W. J. Carpender, who would go on to head the Radiation Therapy Division at the University of Chicago, offered to arrange for a meeting room at the Quadrangle Club at the University of Chicago the next year during the 1957 meeting of the RSNA, so that a scientific discussion could take place following a dinner meeting.[16] The attendees also instructed del Regato to look at the feasibility of having a second annual dinner meeting in conjunction with the annual spring meeting of the American Radium Society. This spring meeting would be held in Quebec City in June 1957.

Fits and Starts

The high hopes for a new organization for radiotherapists stalled in 1957. The American Radium Society meeting in June started out well with most of the North American members of the International Club of Radiotherapists, along with about fifteen other US and Canadian radiotherapists enjoying a fresh lobster dinner at the *Club Universitaire* in Quebec City. Jean Bouchard of Montreal helped organize the meeting, which he thought worthwhile for the social interchange, especially among the large contingent of ICR members.

The meeting, however, was marred by tragedy. The next day, June 2, 1957, Lewis Haas, a Chicago radiotherapist, stopped his car on the road to Ste. Anne de Beaupre to take photographs. As he framed a picture, Haas was struck by a speeding car on the narrow highway and killed instantly. A Hungarian, he had lost most of his immediate family during the Nazi Holocaust. Back home in Illinois, he had done pioneering work with the Betatron at the University of Illinois.[17]

Events went from bad to worse later in the year. The RSNA, which had been meeting in Chicago early in December each year since the end of World War II, changed the meeting date of its annual conference to early November. RSNA's annual meeting had been growing by leaps and bounds, and RSNA's Board of Directors were experimenting with an earlier meeting to see if it could free up hotel rooms in Chicago.[18]

Unfortunately, the news of the date change for the RSNA meeting had slipped past del Regato and J. W. J. Carpender, the ones who were to be responsible for the dinner and scientific meeting for radiotherapists at Chicago's University Club. As a result, del Regato had accepted an engagement in Hawaii in early November, and Carpender was unable to secure the Quadrangle Club for a meeting.

The 1957 meeting of radiotherapists took place on November 1 in a ballroom at the Palmer House. Only twenty-four radiotherapists and three guests attended. Those who did attend, including Fletcher, Garcia, and Schulz, had a forceful discussion about the future of the meetings. All agreed that periodic gatherings and discussions were important for their professional development. The younger radiotherapists questioned that their position as invited guests of ICR members made them feel like second-class citizens. However, the ICR members feared that the protection of the

International Club of Radiotherapists could be lost if the US radiotherapists went off in their own direction.[19]

For del Regato, the discussions at the November 1, 1957, dinner meeting were enough to justify further planning. "These considerations led (him), after due consultation with other members of the International Club, to present at the next meeting a plan for an American Club of Therapeutic Radiologists, definitely not a new society, and with a minimum of formality," del Regato wrote in the record of proceedings leading up to the foundation of the club.[20]

Victor Marcial, a founding member of the club.

1958—"A Maximum of Simplicity"

Five months later, on March 29, 1958, del Regato brought together forty prominent American radiotherapists for lunch at the Hollywood Beach Hotel in Hollywood, Florida. The radiotherapists in the Florida hotel banquet room that noon had just left the business session of the annual meeting of the American Radium Society.[21]

This time, the meeting was about the future of American radiotherapy, and not fellowship. Del Regato presented his blueprint for an American club of radiotherapists, modeled on the existing International Club of Radiotherapists. The plan, he later wrote, "proposed a maximum of simplicity and a minimum of formality: A president in charge of meetings, a secretary in charge of correspondence and arrangements, and a membership committee in charge of eligibility: No dues, two lunch or dinner gatherings every year."[22]

Del Regato brought up three issues that needed to be resolved. The group had to agree on membership criteria, a method for electing officers and the criteria for establishing a quorum.[23]

The discussion, which lasted well over an hour, went back and forth. In general, the representatives of the American chapter of the ICR urged caution. James J. Nickson, from Memorial Hospital in New York, suggested postponing the founding of the club for a year to allow for consultation with ICR. Robert A. Caulk of Washington, DC, and J. W. J. Carpender, both ICR members like Nickson, agreed. Several of those in attendance voiced concern that an American club would become just another lobbying group.[24]

But there were others who were equally committed to creating a stand-alone organization that would be able to represent the interests of US and Canadian radiotherapists. Victor Marcial pointed out that the bonding afforded by a club would be particularly beneficial for younger radiotherapists.

Eligibility, however, would prove to be one of the new organization's biggest stumbling blocks. When it was suggested that the proposed club extend eligibility to "anyone interested in radiotherapy," del Regato weighed in on the side of limiting membership to those who made a full-time living off the practice of radiotherapy. He estimated there were no more than one hundred radiotherapists practicing full time in the United States and approximately fifty in Canada.[25]

Logo of the American Radium Society, which was organized in 1916.

Simeon T. Cantril, founding member and first president of the American Club of Therapeutic Radiologists.

To get consensus on the thorny issue of membership eligibility, del Regato, after consultation with others, appointed Manual Garcia, Milford Schultz, and Simeon Cantril as a steering committee to study the matter further and report its findings at the November meeting in Chicago.[26]

The Founders Agreement

Nearly sixty people crowded into the Chicago Room of the Palmer House on the evening of November 18, 1958, for the first meeting of the American Club of Therapeutic Radiologists. The room was in the basement, immediately adjacent to the kitchen, and there was no little dismay that speakers had to compete with the noise from next door. "After some preliminary horseplay," the minutes noted, "the meeting was called to order."[27] Manuel Garcia, the chairman of the Steering Committee, asked Simeon Cantril to read the one-page Founders Agreement.

That agreement had been hammered out in a dinner meeting at the Shoreham Hotel in Washington, DC, six weeks before. The participants were del Regato, Schulz, and Nickson. Nickson was there to replace Cantril, who was unable to attend.[28]

The Founders Agreement was a remarkably simple document. It noted that the club was established for the purposes of "promoting frequent interchange of ideas among its members and to forward the practice of radiotherapy." The document limited membership to "physicians specializing in therapeutic radiology." Membership nominations were subject to review by all members; more than ten unfavorable votes were sufficient to deny membership to a candidate. Therapeutic radiologists from Canada and Latin America were required to attend two meetings as guests of existing members before applying for membership. Members whose professional practice changed so that they no longer limited their practice to radiotherapy were expected to resign.[29]

The Founders Agreement provided for meeting once or twice a year, "preferably upon the occasion of the annual meetings of the American Radium Society and of the Radiological Society of North America." Members were allowed to bring one guest to each meeting, including residents-in-training in radiology.[30]

Election of officers would be conducted at the November meeting, held in conjunction with the RSNA's annual conference. There were only three officers, a president, vice-president, and secretary. The president was chair of the Membership Committee, and the secretary was custodian of the club's documents. Although the club had no dues in the beginning, the secretary was empowered to assess the members a fee to defray any expenses. Amendments to the Founders Agreement required only an absolute majority of the whole membership to be put into place.[31]

The Largest Gathering of Therapeutic Radiologists in the United States

Ratification of the Founders Agreement at the dinner meeting on November 18, 1958, was relatively swift. There were a few questions and comments. Bernard Roswit of New York suggested that the club call itself the Pan-American Club of Therapeutic Radiologists to include radiotherapists from Canada, Central and South America for membership. Herman Suit, then at NCI in Bethesda, echoed Roswit, wondering why the organization was called the "American" Club if it restricted membership to the United States. One doctor questioned why it was a club rather than a society.[32] Members were assured that membership was not restricted to US applicants but rather that requirements were different for non-US applicants.

Del Regato patiently explained that there was already an ICR, and that the purpose of the club was to provide a forum for radiotherapists from the United States to meet on a regular basis. He went on to say that the Founders Agreement made provision for membership of Canadian and Latin American radiotherapists. The word *Club* was selected, del Regato said, to reflect the organization's informality.

With these explanations out of the way, Jesshill Love from Louisville who was chairing the organizational meeting of the club, called for a vote on the Founders Agreement. Following approval by unanimous acclamation, Milford Shulz read a list of the first ninety-two founding members of the club. Del Regato then announced that an additional nineteen applications had been received and would be voted upon as soon as the membership elected a slate of officers. Garcia and E. M. Japha moved that the new applicants be considered founding members.[33]

Once that motion had been unanimously approved, Garcia quickly turned to the nominations presented by the Steering Committee. Simeon T. Cantril was nominated for the presidency, J. W. J. Carpender was put forth as the club's vice-presidential candidate, and del Regato was suggested as ACTR's first secretary.[34]

Garcia solicited additional nominations from the floor, only to be met by a cry to close the nominations and vote. Like everything else that occurred that evening, the election of the ACTR's first slate of officers was unanimous.[35]

It remained for Henry Kaplan to remind the new members of the serious purposes for which the club was being formed. Kaplan spoke of his fervent hope that special scientific subjects would be chosen for discussion at future meetings. John T. Mallams of Dallas seconded Kaplan's remarks, suggesting that members be asked to make presentations at future meetings regarding the status of radiotherapy in their regions and states.[36]

Some two hours after the meeting started, Cantril adjourned the gathering. It had taken three years and a great deal of work, but del Regato, Garcia, Schulz, Cantril, Fletcher, Kaplan, Nickson, and others had brought forth an entirely new organization.

For his own sake, del Regato felt a great sense of pride. "This was the largest gathering of radiotherapists in the United States up to this point," he later wrote. "Those present admitted that they had never met many of the others. There was spontaneous warmth and enthusiasm surpassing our own expectations."[37]

Endnotes

1. Bill Beck Tape-recorded Telephone Oral History Interview with Donn Mosser, Minneapolis, Minnesota, April 2, 2007.

2. *American Radium Society*, "About the ARS," http://www.americanradiumsociety. org.

3. Juan A. del Regato, "The American Board of Radiology: Its 50ᵗʰ Anniversary," *American Journal of Radiology*, vol. 144, January 1985, pp. 197–200

4. Bill Beck Interview with Luther Brady and Seymour Leavitt, p. 2.

5. David Hussey Tape-recorded Telephone Oral History Interview with Philip Rubin, Rochester, New York, October 7, 2003, p. 7.

6. *American Radium Society*, "About the ARS," http://www.americanradiumsociety. org.

7. *About RSNA: History of the Radiological Society of North America*, "Part 8, The Golden Era," http://www.rsna.org/About/history/articles.cfm.

8. Ibid.

9. In Montgomery, Alabama, that week, a civil rights worker activist and domestic by the name of Rosa Parks was issued a citation for refusing to give up her seat to a white man and move to the back of a city bus. On the evening that ten radiotherapists and their guests gathered at Barney's in Chicago on December 5, 1955, Dr. Martin Luther King, Jr., a young Baptist preacher in Montgomery, proclaimed a bus boycott in the former capital of the Confederacy. Montgomery Bus Boycott would be the opening curtain on a twenty-year civil rights struggle that would transform American society. Clifton Daniel, ed., *Chronicle of the Twentieth Century* (Mt. Kisco, New York: Chronicle Publications, 1988), p. 774.

10. *Record of Proceedings, American Club of Therapeutic Radiologists*, "Preamble," December 15 [sic], 1955, p. A.

11. Bill Beck Tape-recorded Telephone Oral History Interview with Bill Moss, Lake Oswego, Oregon, November 9, 2006, p. 2.

12. *Record of Proceedings, American Club of Therapeutic Radiologists*, "Preamble," December 15 [sic], 1955, p. A.

13. *Record of Proceedings, American Club of Therapeutic Radiologists*, December 6, 1956, p. B.

14. Ibid.

15. Bill Beck Tape-recorded Telephone Oral History Interview with Bill Moss, Lake Oswego, Oregon, November 9, 2006, p. 2.

16. *Record of Proceedings, American Club of Therapeutic Radiologists*, December 6, 1956, p. B.

17. *Record of Proceedings, American Club of Therapeutic Radiologists*, June 1, 1957, n.p.

18. *About RSNA: History of the Radiological Society of North America*, Part 8, "The Golden Era," http://www.rsna.org/About/history/articles.cfm.

19. *Record of Proceedings, American Club of Therapeutic Radiologists*, November 1, 1957, p. 1D.

20. Ibid.

21. *Record of Proceedings, American Club of Therapeutic Radiologists*, March 29, 1958, p. 1.

22. Ibid., p. 2.

23. Ibid.

24. Ibid.

25. Ibid.

26. Ibid.

27. *Record of Proceedings, American Club of Therapeutic Radiologists*, November 18, 1958, p. 6.

28. *Record of Proceedings, American Club of Therapeutic Radiologists*, October 1, 1958, p. 3.

29. *Record of Proceedings, American Club of Therapeutic Radiologists*, "Founders Agreement," p. 5.

30. Ibid.

31. Ibid.

32. *Record of Proceedings, American Club of Therapeutic Radiologists*, November 18, 1958, p. 6.

33. Ibid., p. 7.

34. Ibid.

35. Ibid.

36. Ibid.

37. Ibid.

The first ASTRO Gold Medalists in 1977: Gilbert H. Fletcher, Juan A. del Regato, and Henry S. Kaplan.

CHAPTER THREE

The ASTRO Triad

ASTRO's roots date back slightly more than a half-century. It all began in the mid-1950s, when America's radiotherapists started gathering at a Chicago restaurant each November or December while attending the annual meeting of the Radiological Society of North America (RSNA). In 1955, some of the most important people practicing radiation therapy in the United States met at Barney's Market Club on Randolph Street. Thus was formed the nucleus for what would become the largest and most influential society of radiation oncologists in the world.

The status of postgraduate radiotherapy in the United States was fairly limited in the mid-1950s. Indeed, there were very few physicians who devoted their practice in the 1950s solely to therapeutic radiology. Early radiotherapy equipment caused such toxicity that the utility of radiotherapy had been in serious question in the 1920s and 1930s. At the time, there were no medical oncologists either. Most cancer treatments with radiation therapy were given by general radiologists, most of whom practiced both therapy and diagnosis. The few who limited their practice to therapeutic radiology in the 1950s would meet informally at RSNA and the ARS, and it was there that the idea of a separate organization for therapeutic radiology first surfaced.

The Three Giants

When ASTRO made the decision in 1976 to begin awarding Gold Medals for outstanding achievement in the field of radiotherapy, the first three medals were awarded to Juan A. del Regato, Gilbert H. Fletcher, and Henry S. Kaplan in the same year. It is generally conceded that each of them would have preferred to have been the sole recipient that year. Robert Parker, ASTRO's immediate past president and chairman of the ASTRO Board, was asked to contact the three honorees and inform them their selection.

"I called Dr. Fletcher," Parker recalled, "and he said, 'That's nice. Give my third of a medal to Dr. del Regato.'"[32] And Kaplan said he was far too busy to attend a meeting just to receive a medal.[33]

The response was typical of Fletcher, the sometimes acerbic, sometimes argumentative head of therapeutic radiology at Houston's M. D. Anderson Cancer Hospital. It was Fletcher's brilliance in the field of radiation oncology, however, that earned him a place in the triad of physicians whose careers had such an impact on the field of radiotherapy and on the formation and early years of ASTRO, in particular.

Parker never found out exactly what transpired, but del Regato evidently was on the phone to Fletcher and Kaplan urging them to participate in the awards ceremony. Within thirty minutes of his calls to Fletcher and Kaplan, both called Parker to say that they would be at the meeting to accept the inaugural ASTRO Gold Medal. To his dying day, Parker prized the photograph in his possession of what he called "the three giants in radiation oncology" standing side by side with their medals at the ceremony.[34]

Del Regato, Fletcher, and Kaplan were never particularly close, although they had a great deal of mutual respect. Fletcher and del Regato grew to like each other in their later years. Even today, fifty years after the founding of the International Club of Radiologists, leading radiation oncologists identify with one of the traditions established by del Regato, Fletcher, and Kaplan, and the schools with which they were identified continue a friendly rivalry. Contemporaries hazard the guess, however, that the first time that the three ever stood shoulder-to-shoulder for a photograph was on the occasion of the award of the first ASTRO Gold Medals in 1977. Collectively, they shaped the practice of radiotherapy in the United States—and the future course of ASTRO.

The staff of the Chicago Tumor Institute in 1938. Henri Coutard is fourth from the left, and Juan del Regato is second from the right, both in the front row.

Cancer, *by Juan del Regato,*
first published in 1947.

Juan A. del Regato (1909–1999)

Juan A. del Regato, MD, is one of the most revered physicians in the history of American Radiotherapy. One of his greatest contributions to radiation oncology was in education. A pioneer in the training of radiation oncologists in the United States, del Regato succeeded in identifying therapeutic radiology as a separate medical specialty through his able and indefatigable efforts spanning more than a half-century. In 1949, he established the first training center in the United States dedicated to therapeutic radiology.[3]

Del Regato was born in Camaguey, Cuba, on March 1, 1909, the son of a film projectionist and photographer.[4] For the 1926–1927 term, he enrolled at the University of Havana in a seven-year program for a medical degree. By the 1929–1930 school term, he was a first-year medical student and a student intern at the Institute del Cancer of Havana. Having some knowledge of photography, he was offered a job in the X-ray Department at the Calixto Garcia Cancer Hospital. When del Regato replied that he didn't know anything about radiology, the director shot back. "Damn it," he said. "I didn't ask you if you knew anything! I asked you if you wanted the job!"[5] The "job" turned out to be relieving the diagnostic radiologist by doing all the roentgentherapy with a 200 kV Coolidge tube.

In 1930, political unrest forced the University of Havana to close all the educational facilities and disperse the student body. The physicians of the *Cuban Liga Contra El Cancer* decided to send del Regato to Paris to complete his medical training, since Paris had already agreed to take transfers from the University of Havana.[6] Because of his interest and experience in radiotherapy, del Regato was given a letter of introduction to Claudius Regaud, the director of the Radium Institute at the *Fondation Curie* in Paris. While attending medical school from 1930 to 1934, del Regato spent his free time and vacations at the Institute.

Then upon graduation in 1934, he became a house officer/resident/fellow in the Department of Roentgentherapy under Claudius Regaud (1870–1940), Antoine Lacassagne (1884–1971), and Henri Coutard (1876–1950), the legendary triumvirate of the Radium Institute. These three illustrious radiation oncologists became del Regato's mentors between 1934 and 1938. While in Paris, del Regato completed his MD thesis in 1937. He eventually became the assistant to Coutard, who in 1932 had treated the American mining millionaire Spencer Penrose (1867–1939) for laryngeal cancer.

At the Radium Institute in Paris, del Regato designed one of the first collimators, with a lighting device that defined where an X-ray beam will enter the skin.[7] In 1937, after receiving his MD degree in France, del Regato took a year of fellowship in radiation therapy at the *Fondation Curie*.[8] Lacassagne appointed del Regato as an assistant to Coutard.

In the fall of 1937, Coutard agreed to accept Robert Millikan's invitation to go to the Kellogg Radiation Laboratory of the California Institute of Technology in Pasadena. After six months in Pasadena he joined Max Cutler of Michael Reese Hospital in Chicago and helped with the foundation of the ill-fated and short-lived Chicago Tumor Institute.[9] Coutard asked del Regato to join him in the Windy City in 1938 where del Regato's main obligation was to teach six-week courses on the treatment of cancer. Dozens of physicians from surrounding states came to Chicago for the courses. While del Regato was in Chicago, he became curious as to how many physicians practiced radiotherapy exclusively in the United States. After much difficulty in acquiring data, he counted a total of thirty-nine.[10]

Early Days at NCI

In 1940, del Regato became a research fellow at the recently created National Cancer Institute (NCI). The NCI did not yet have radiotherapy equipment in Bethesda, Maryland, but instead had a radiotherapy clinic at the US Marine Hospital in Baltimore. Del Regato and his wife, Inez, were in Baltimore when the Japanese attacked Pearl Harbor on December 7, 1941, and his work at NCI took a backseat to other war work.

Ellis Fischel

Staff and material shortages were considerable because of the war, and in 1943, del Regato was asked to take the position as head radiotherapist at the Ellis Fischel State Cancer Hospital in Columbia, Missouri.[11] Because of the war, like many other medical facilities at the time, the hospital had lost most of its staff.[12]

During his early years in practice, del Regato became convinced that failures in the treatment of cancer were often due to the inadequate preparation and information obtained by physicians who first saw and advised the patients. He saw a need for a text providing realistic information on differential diagnoses, indications for curative treatment and prognoses. With that in mind, del Regato began collecting appropriate illustrations and references and he developed an outline for a one-volume book for general practitioners and students, a book that would give equal emphasis to pathology, surgery and radiotherapy techniques.[13] He engaged Missouri pathologist, Laurence Vedder Ackerman, to write the book with him. *Cancer: Diagnosis, Treatment and Prognosis* was first published in 1947 and went into multiple editions into the 1970s.

Penrose

Del Regato's success at Ellis Fischel brought him to the attention of wealthy philanthropists such as Julie Penrose, who visited the hospital in 1948. She was impressed with the work of the institution in caring for the state's cancer patients so she decided to build a similar hospital in Colorado Springs, Colorado, in memory of her late husband, Spencer. She invited del Regato to come and direct it.

Spencer Penrose had made a fortune in Colorado gold mines in the Cripple Creek District during the 1890s. During the twentieth century, Penrose and his wife, Julie, had spent millions to develop their hometown

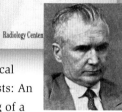

Radiological Oncologists: An Unfolding of a Medical Specialty *by Juan del Regato, 1993.*

A group of Penrose residents in 1966. Left to right: James Cox, G. Stephen Brown, J. Frank Wilson, V. Perez, and Charles G. Taggart.

One of the many Visiting Professor Seminars held at Penrose between 1949 and 1974. Sitting left to right: C. Chahbazian, M. Berthong, L. Ackerman, J. A. del Regato, and R. Perez-Tamayo; standing, left to right: D. Dawson, G. S. Brown, E. Nava, V. Periz, A. Gutierrez, R. Kagan, and G. Taylor.

of Colorado Springs.[14] When Penrose developed esophageal cancer in 1938, he arranged for the installation of a 400-kVp General Electric Maximar unit at El Pomar, his Colorado Springs mountain estate, and hired Coutard to administer the treatments. Penrose died the next year. His widow, Julie, then built the Penrose Tumor Clinic at the city's Glockner Hospital, and Coutard stayed on as the clinic's first radiotherapist.[15]

Julie Penrose expanded the clinic into a full-fledged cancer hospital in 1948. Coutard recommended his former student in Missouri, del Regato, as a candidate to head the proposed Penrose Cancer Hospital. Early in 1949, del Regato arrived in Colorado Springs to become the director of the new hospital, and Coutard returned to France in the fall of 1949, where he died the following year.[16]

Del Regato was an elegant and prolific writer, and his books on the nation's radiation physicists and radiation oncologists are recommended reading for each succeeding generation of those entering the field. He trained dozens of residents who would later aspire to leadership roles in ASTR and ASTRO. His interest in historical preservation created a documentary record of radiation therapy for future generations. In the 1960s, he initiated the first clinical, multi-institutional protocol study on prostate treatment.

By the mid-1950s, del Regato was convinced that the growing practice of radiotherapy needed a way for radiotherapists to gather at least annually to discuss items of mutual concern, enhance their education, report scientific advances, and socialize with their peers.

In 1955, del Regato hosted the meeting at Barney's Market Club to discuss the formation of such an organization. His concept was the origin of the American Society for Therapeutic Radiology and Oncology. After years of nurturing the growth of the organization, del Regato accepted the presidency of ASTR in 1974.

Juan del Regato died in Michigan in 1999 at the age of ninety.

Gilbert H. Fletcher (1911–1992)

Gilbert Fletcher was born in Paris in 1911, the son of Marie Auspel of Auvergne and of Walter Scott Fletcher (1872–1914), a wealthy American businessman residing in France. Walter Fletcher was from Springfield, Massachusetts, and the son of a Civil War veteran and Protestant minister. He made his fortune in the export/import business of ladies notions and died in 1914 when young Gilbert was only three years old, leaving a trust fund in New York City.

After graduating from a private high school in Paris in 1929, Fletcher registered at the Sorbonne to study Latin, Greek, and philosophy. His older brother then moved the family business to Belgium, and Gilbert switched to a bachelor's degree in engineering and obtained his degree at the University of Louvain in 1932. Afterwards, he attended the University of Brussels, where he earned a master's degree in mathematics in 1935 and completed course work for a doctorate in physics in 1937.

Rather than complete his PhD thesis, he entered the Brussels medical school (1937–1941). Fletcher had become the proverbial peripatetic perpetual student, and his family complained. However, during his junior year Fletcher rotated through the university cancer clinics, which were heavily endowed with radium from the Belgian Congo.

Fletcher graduated from medical school in June 1941. At the time, Louvain was occupied by the Nazis. He had dual American and French citizenships, an American passport, and a trust fund in New York, which was now cut off. If war was declared between Germany and America, he might be incarcerated. Fletcher escaped to America by walking through occupied France and then unoccupied (Vichy) France, traveling all the way to Lisbon. He went on to the United States by freighter, arriving in New York in January 1942.[17]

After a few months of training in gynecology at the French Hospital in New York City, Fletcher began training in general radiology at the New York Hospital in 1942. There he met and later married Mary Walker Critz from Mississippi, who was in New York for a residency in ophthalmology. Fletcher was certified in general radiology by the American Board of Radiology in 1945. From March 1945 to March 1947 Fletcher served the US Army at the Pittsburgh VA Hospital doing upper GI series X-ray exams.

When he was discharged from the service, he and Mary decided to settle in the South. Mary Fletcher had Mississippi connections with R. Lee Clark, who was at the time recruiting staff for a new cancer hospital in Houston. Clark offered Fletcher a position in the radiology department at

Gilbert H. Fletcher at an M. D. Anderson Planning Clinic.

36

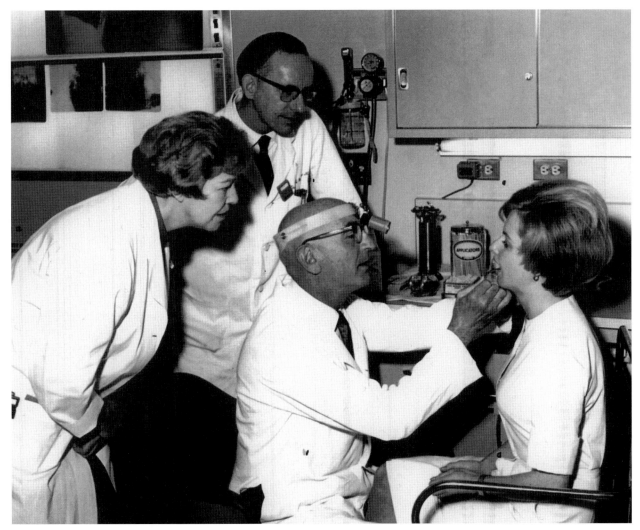

Gilbert Fletcher examining a patient at the M. D. Anderson Planning Clinic with Norah duV. Tapley and Max Boone looking on.

the new hospital. Before accepting a position at what would soon become the M. D. Anderson Cancer Center, Fletcher decided to do a fellowship in radiotherapy, so he spent several months as an observer in Paris, Stockholm, London, and Manchester. This was probably a critical period in Fletcher's career. He later told associates he was particularly impressed with Baclesse and Patterson. Upon his return to the United States in January 1948, Fletcher accepted an appointment as head of the Department of Radiology at M. D. Anderson Cancer Center, with responsibilities in both radiodiagnosis (until 1963) and radiotherapy.

Early in his professional career, Gilbert Fletcher established himself as one of the great leaders in radiation therapy. He revolutionized the conceptual basis of the field and established a methodology of treatment that is now practiced around the world. His personal contributions are too numerous to list comprehensively here. There are two major areas, however, that must be mentioned—technological innovation and the establishment of a firm scientific rationale for radiotherapy.

In 1950, Fletcher and Leonard Grimmett, a teleradium physicist he recruited to M. D. Anderson, designed the first cobalt-60 teletherapy unit.

Also in the 1950s, he designed the prototype of the Fletcher-Suit-Delclos system for intracavitary gynecological brachytherapy. In the 1960s, he and Norah duV. Tapley investigated the applications of electron beam therapy, and in subsequent years, he participated in the first nationwide trials of hyperbaric oxygen and of fast neutron therapy.

Even more important for posterity were Fletcher's contributions to clinical research through a systematic analysis of causes of failure and complications in patients treated in a disciplined and consistent way. This led to continuous refinement of the "Fletcher school" of cancer treatment. His analysis of the dose required for tumor control led to the establishment in the late 1960s of the concept of "subclinical disease" which showed that subclinical deposits of cancer could be eradicated with lower doses of radiation than would be required for gross tumor masses. This concept provided a rationale for the shrinking field technique and the use of a combination of radiotherapy and surgery for organ preservation.

H. Rodney Withers and Gilbert Fletcher at an ASTRO social event.

Lester Peters, who followed Fletcher as chairman of Radiation Therapy at M. D. Anderson Cancer Center, recently noted that "although Fletcher was never a laboratory researcher himself, he understood the importance of radiobiological research in advancing clinical practice. In 1959 he set up a Section of Experimental Radiotherapy at M. D. Anderson, a laboratory originally led by Herman Suit and later by H. Rodney Withers and Luka Milas. Peters pointed out that "it is a tribute to his belief in the value of radiobiological research that the intimate relationship he fostered between the laboratory and the clinic has continued and prospered to the present day."

In 1963 the Committee for Radiation Therapy Studies (CRTS), which later became the Committee for Radiation Oncology Studies (CROS), was established by Ken Endicott under a grant of the National Cancer Institute. It was formed to serve as an aid to the National Advisory Cancer Subcommittee for Diagnosis and Treatment on matters related to radiation therapy. Gilbert Fletcher was selected to chair this committee for almost a decade. The CRTS/CROS was responsible for many of the advances in radiobiology, physics, and radiation therapy in the 1960s and 1970s, including the establishment of training grants for radiation oncology residents and radiobiology graduate students.

Fletcher was a prodigious writer. He was author or co-author of 372 scientific papers between 1947 and 1972, three editions of his classic *Textbook of Radiotherapy,* and three other books on head and neck cancer. Half of Fletcher's scientific papers were coauthored, indicating his interest in collaborating with peers and with residents.

The University of Texas M. D. Anderson Hospital clinical radiotherapy staff in 1963. First row, left to right: L. Miller, F. Alaniz-Camino, G. H. Fletcher, and P. Chau; second row, left to right: T. Ilos, T. Watanavit, R. Zimmerman, and R. Lindberg; third row, left to right: H. Suit, H. Hyholth, and unidentified dental service representative.

Gilbert H. Fletcher Society Membership, 1976.

Fletcher was one of the great teachers of radiotherapy. He was responsible for the training of more than two hundred residents during his career. In 1975, his trainees founded the Gilbert H. Fletcher Society to provide a venue for scientific and social interchange among those who were trained by him and their trainees.

Peters recalled that "Fletcher was a man who held definite opinions and he would defend these opinions aggressively. Yet when he faced convincing evidence, he was always willing to change his mind on the basis of facts rather than ideology."

Joe Castro, who completed his radiation oncology residency at M. D. Anderson, remembered Fletcher saying to him, "Look, it takes five to eight years to learn your trade. That was the way he described it, a trade."[18]

In the late 1960s and early 1970s, M. D. Anderson was still small enough that residents and interns could get to know most of the staff very well. Castro recalled that Fletcher "had assembled a super roster of people. So first of all, you had this incredible faculty, and then there was a steady stream of trainees coming through. It was just about that time that M. D. Anderson began a four-year training program in radiation oncology."[19]

Castro also recalled that "the list of people who Gilbert Fletcher trained is very long and very illustrious in the field of clinical research, and that's what he was interested in, and that's what he tried to drum into you."[20]

Bob Lindberg, who was trained by del Regato and was on the faculty in Fletcher's department for many years, was once asked his assessment of these two giants of American radiotherapy. His response was simple, yet eloquent. "Del Regato taught me the art of radiotherapy," Lindberg said, "and Fletcher taught me the science of radiotherapy!"

Fletcher was a founding member of the International Club of Radiotherapists in 1953, president of the American Radium Society (ARS) in 1963 and of ASTR in 1967. During his career he earned the Antoine Béclère Medal and the Medal of Honor from the American Cancer Society, as well as Gold Medals from the ARS (the Janeway Medal), the RSNA and ASTRO. Fletcher died in Houston of heart failure and leukemia on January 11, 1992.[21]

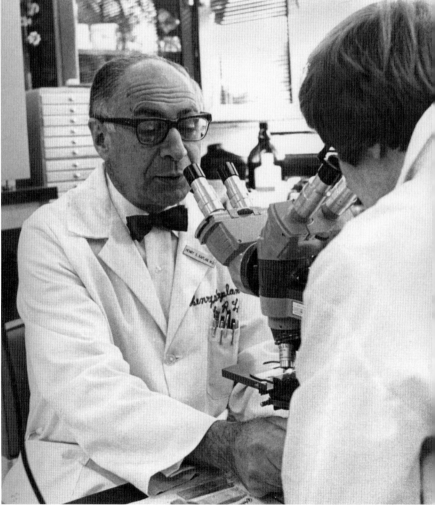

Henry S. Kaplan at the microscope.

Henry S. Kaplan (1918–1984)

Henry Seymour Kaplan was the only native-born American among the three giants who dominated modern American radiotherapy in the middle years of the twentieth century. He was born in Chicago on April 24, 1918. After receiving a BS degree from the University of Chicago, he earned his MD degree from Rush Medical College in 1940. Kaplan served an internship at Michael Reese Hospital, where he met Max Cutler, head of the Chicago Tumor Institute. He then went to Minneapolis for a fellowship in general radiology under Leo Rigler at the University of Minnesota. While there, he became acquainted further with radiation therapy when he studied under the physicist, Karl Stenstrom.

While in training with Rigler, Kaplan reported on a study of the early detection of cancer of the stomach.[22] He was certified in general radiology by the American Board of Radiology in 1944 and took a position as an instructor and later assistant professor at Yale University Medical School.[23] In

E. Dale Trout
(1901-1977)

Although not one of the American Club's founding members, E. Dale Trout was in on the planning for its establishment from the very beginning.

At the time that Juan del Regato, Gilbert Fletcher, Henry Kaplan, James Nickson, Manuel Garcia, Milford Schulz, and others were laying the groundwork for the American Club of Therapeutic Radiology, E. Dale Trout was General Electric's liaison with the nation's radiotherapy community. From his offices and laboratory in Milwaukee, Trout kept his finger on the pulse of North American developments in X-ray equipment and techniques. Del Regato and the founders had a great deal of respect for Trout and his knowledge of the equipment that made the industry possible.

Born and raised in the tiny farming community of Franklin, Indiana, south of Indianapolis on November 3, 1901, he earned his BS degree at Franklin College in 1922 and spent the next six years teaching high school science in Indiana. In 1928, Trout joined the staff of the Victor X-Ray Company in Chicago, then one of the major manufacturers of X-ray tubes.[1] In early 1930, General Electric purchased Victor X-Ray Company and later moved the firm's operations to GE laboratories in Milwaukee, Wisconsin.[2]

By the time Trout retired from GE in 1962, he had spent a lifetime evaluating X-ray equipment and its performance, safety factors and protective devices. Along the way, Trout made major contributions to the science of radiotherapy and met virtually every practicing radiotherapist in North America. In 1952, his alma mater, Franklin College, awarded Trout an honorary doctor of science degree.[3]

At many of the early dinners to plan the formation of the American Club, Trout was an honored guest. When the first Executive Committee needed money to print a membership directory, Trout arranged for an "angel," the General Electric Milwaukee labs, to fund the project.[4]

General Electric consultant E. Dale Trout, a respected physicist who knew everybody in the field of radiotherapy.

Following retirement, Trout embarked upon a second career that kept him at the forefront of development in American radiotherapy. In 1962, Trout joined the faculty of Oregon State University as professor of radiologic physics. He established the X-ray Science and Engineering Laboratory at Corvallis and also carried an appointment as professor of clinical radiology at the University of Oregon's medical school.

Donn Mosser met Trout for the first time at the 1955 founders' dinner at Barney's Market Club in Chicago. "Dale Trout was short and stocky and very affable," Mosser recalled. "He went to Oregon State after he retired and taught physics. He knew just about everybody in radiotherapy in the 1950s and 1960s."[5]

When Trout died of a myocardial infarction in early 1977, shortly after retiring from his second career, his hometown newspaper, the *Corvallis Gazette-Times*, eulogized Trout as a "wise and witty man." The editorial writer described him as "an unassuming man," but one who "was known worldwide as an expert in the field of X-ray science and radiation. He was a fixture at every major US space shot and designed some of the experiments carried out by American astronauts."[6]

In many of his early novels, the late Hoosier writer Kurt Vonnegut included a mad scientist character by the name of Kilgore Trout. Vonnegut worked in GE's public relations office following World War II and would have known of Trout's reputation inside the company. And Vonnegut grew up in Indianapolis, twenty miles north of Trout's Franklin hometown.

If he had ever made the connection, Dale Trout would likely have gotten a huge kick from the irony of it all.

Endnotes

1. *American Journal of Roentgenology*, "E. Dale Trout 1901-1977," http://www.ajronline.org/cgi/

2. "Mobilizing for Cancer," *Time*, September 29, 1930.

3. *American Journal of Roentgenology*, "E. Dale Trout 1901-1977," http://www.ajronline.org/cgi/

4. Record of Proceedings, American Club of Therapeutic Radiologists, April 8, 1959, p. 9.

5. Bill Beck tape-recorded Telephone Oral History Interview with Donn Mosser, Minneapolis, Minnesota, April 2, 2007, p. 4.

6. "A Wise and Witty Man," *Corvallis Gazette-Times*, February 3, 1977.

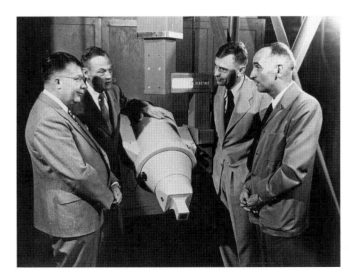

Dale Trout (left), longtime General Electric consultant, discusses M. D. Anderson's GE cobalt-60 unit in 1951 with (left to right) William G. Pollard, PhD, executive director of ORINS; Marshall Brucer; and Gilbert H. Fletcher.

Stanford physicist Edward Ginzton and Henry S. Kaplan.

New Haven, he pursued his interests in diagnostic radiology, but then he took a fellowship to do basic sciences research at the NCI. While he was in Bethesda, Kaplan did original work on leukemia induction in mice. For the rest of his life, Kaplan maintained close contact with NCI and its decision-makers.

At the age of thirty, he was offered the position of professor of radiology and chairman of the department at Stanford University School of Medicine in 1948, then located in San Francisco. Kaplan accepted the challenge and chose to emphasize the importance of research to the development of radiology as a specialty. Over the next quarter century, Kaplan made significant contributions in the basic sciences and clinical practice of radiation therapy and achieved an undisputed position of leadership among radiation oncologists.[24]

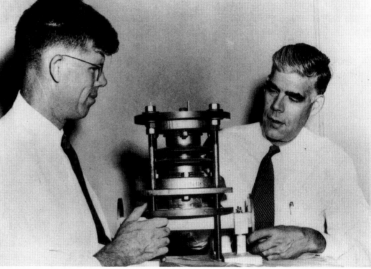

Russell and Sigurd Varian with their klystron in 1939.

He and Morton Kligerman were largely responsible for NCI's generous support of radiotherapy training and research during the 1960s and 1970s. In the early 1960s, Kaplan at Stanford and Kligerman at Yale were successful in establishing the first NCI-funded, four-year training programs in radiation therapy, which included a year of laboratory research.

At Stanford, Kaplan quickly established his leadership skills. He was prominent in the decision to move the hospital and school to the Palo Alto campus in 1959. He helped select the new hospital's architect, Edward Durrell Stone, and he was influential in establishing a basic research direction at the school. His role in the recruitment of Arthur Kornberg and

Joshua Lederberg, both of whom became Nobel laureates, created a lasting legacy for the school.

Shortly after arriving at Stanford, Kaplan learned of the work being done on the university campus by Edward Ginzton and associates at the microwave laboratories. Microwave technology had been essential to the development of radar at the outset of World War II, and Stanford researchers subsequently applied the technology to linear accelerators for physics research.

Kaplan envisioned the application of this technology to cancer treatment. Similar research was being conducted in the United Kingdom, where the world's first medical linear accelerator, powered by a magnetron, was installed for patient treatment in 1953. The Stanford device, powered by a klystron and developed by Edward Ginzton and collaborators Paul Howard-Flanders and brothers Russell and Sigurd Varian, was installed at the Stanford-Lane Hospital in San Francisco in 1956. Malcolm A. Bagshaw, who succeeded Kaplan as department chairman, wrote in a 1984 "Memorial Resolution" to Kaplan: "At his instigation and with his encouragement, the physics team built the first linear accelerator in the western hemisphere tailored expressly for radiotherapy."[25]

Researchers at Stanford enjoyed great success in reporting the utility of the linear accelerator to the treatment of various forms of cancer.[26] The original accelerator, dubbed LA-1, was later moved to the Palo Alto campus and when it was decommissioned it was sent to the Smithsonian Institution in Washington, DC.[27]

Using the medical linear accelerator, Kaplan was able to extend the work of Rene Gilbert of Geneva, Vera Peters from Princess Margaret Hospital in Toronto, and others in revolutionizing the treatment of lymphoma and Hodgkin's disease.

The first model of a Varian medical linear accelerator in 1962.

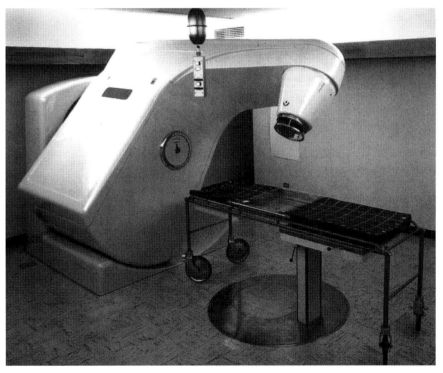

Henry S. Kaplan and Saul Rosenberg.

Hodgkin's Disease *by Henry S. Kaplan, first published in 1972.*

Henry S. Kaplan

Thomas Hodgkin (1798–1866). The original of this portrait hangs in the Gordon Museum, Guy's Hospital and Medical School, London, and is reproduced here by permission of the Curator.

Harvard University Press, Cambridge Massachusetts, 1972

Through his careful study of consecutively treated patients, documenting sites of initial disease and sites of relapse, Kaplan advanced significantly the concepts of treatment for Hodgkin's disease. He documented its contiguity of spread, the necessity to irradiate the adjacent uninvolved lymph node bearing areas, and the use of a tumoricidal dose. Until that time, most patients with Hodgkin's disease had been treated with inadequately small fields and insufficient doses of radiation.

The linac was well suited for treating large contiguous areas to sterilize the tumor locally with moderately high doses of radiation as well as irradiating the surrounding areas. Together with Saul A. Rosenberg, a medical oncologist he recruited to Stanford, Kaplan was among the first to introduce the concept of randomized clinical trials for the lymphomas. Randomized clinical trials soon became the standard for evaluating new cancer therapies. Kaplan authored two editions of a classic historical and technical text on Hodgkin's disease.

In the 1960s, there was a glaring need for training programs for radiation oncologists. Kaplan, who was then a member of the National Cancer Advisory Board, forcefully advocated the extension of federal grants for the establishment of training centers.

"I was part of the first group with Henry Kaplan and Herman Suit to be funded by NCI, first for research training," explained Philip Rubin. "That was the beginning of our residency programs. We had that grant for about ten or fifteen years. It was very important. And Henry Kaplan was a big force at NCI and very significant along with Gilbert Fletcher and Juan del Regato. That funded the residency programs."[28] Kaplan himself was an inspirational teacher, and many of his trainees went on to become national leaders and chairs of prominent Departments of Radiology and Radiation Oncology.

Kaplan also was aware that progress in clinical radiotherapy had been due to an understanding of radiobiology. Early on, he emphasized the role of radiobiological research, including electron beam therapy, radiation sensitizers, and negative pi-mesons.[29]

Kaplan's stature in radiotherapy and his contacts at NCI led to even more research funding in the 1970s. Kaplan had served on the National Cancer Advisory Board in the 1960s and he had the ear of US Representative Paul G. Rogers, chair of the Health Subcommittee of the House Committee on Commerce. Largely through Kaplan's influence, federal legislation led to the concept of a "bypass budget" for the NCI and a bill authorizing support for the development of cancer centers. Rubin noted that "the next thing that happened was radiation research was being promulgated, and a number of us had what we called radiation center grants. They were the academic backbone. Those grants eventually became program project grants, so having education and research supported was extremely important. Those were major building blocks in getting our specialty going and making it what it really is today."[30]

During his career, Kaplan received innumerable honors and awards. He was one of the founders and president of the Radiation Research Society, and he was elected to the National Academy of Science. He was awarded the prestigious *Chevalier de la Legion d'Honneur*, Republic of France, and was the first radiologist elected to the Institute of Medicine. He received the Atoms for Peace Award, the first Charles L. Kettering Award Prize from the General Motors Cancer Foundation and Gold Medals from ASTRO, the ACR, the ARS (Janeway Medal), the American Association for Cancer Research (G. H. A. Clowes Memorial Award) and the Association of University Radiologists. Kaplan was elected president of ASTR in 1966.

Kaplan was a kind and generous person who exhibited great contradictions in his personality. He was feared by many of those around him, yet admired and revered by his associates, most of whom considered him one of the best clinicians and laboratory scientists practicing in the field of radiation oncology. A nonsmoker, he died of lung cancer in California in February 1984.

At his memorial service at Stanford University, tributes were delivered by Donald Kennedy, university president; Vince DeVita, director of the National Cancer Institute; and Ed Ginzton, chairman of the Varian Associates Board. A few weeks before his death, Kaplan made these comments to a campus writer:

I'd like to be remembered for my accomplishments that stand the test of time such as the work on Hodgkin's disease and malignant lymphomas. That is an area where there will be continued further improvement, but I think we contributed a foundation stone which today is leading to the cure worldwide of hundreds of thousands of patients.

I'd like to be remembered as the co-developer of the medical linear accelerator for cancer treatment, which today is a standard of excellence throughout the world. And for developing not just the machine, but the standards for its use.

I'd like to be remembered for my service on the National Cancer Advisory Board in 1960 at a time when the number of radiotherapists in the United States was about 120, and the number of physicians in radiotherapy training was only 18. Today, as a result of these efforts, there are close to 2,000 board-certified radiation therapists.

I'd also like to be remembered as somebody with a reasonably good sense of humor, with a love of art and music and literature, and hopefully as a good husband, a good father, and loyal friend.[31]

Endnotes

1. Bill Beck Tape-recorded Telephone Oral History Interview with Donn Mosser, Minneapolis, Minnesota, April 2, 2007, p. 3.

2. Ibid.

3. Juan A. del Regato, Obituary, *New York Times,* June 22, 1999, p. A29.

4. Juan A. del Regato, *The Unfolding of Therapeutic Radiology in the United States: A Participant's Views and Autobiographical Essay*, p. 197.

5. Ibid.

6. Ibid.

7. Anita J. Latter, "The Making of a Medical Pioneer," *Hospital News & Florida Health Care Report*, April 1996, p. 1.

8. Ibid.

9. www.juanadelregatofoundation.org/pdf.

10. Juan A. del Regato, *The Unfolding of Therapeutic Radiology in the United States: A Participant's Views and Autobiographical Essay*, p. 200.

11. Ibid., p. 201.

12. Ibid., p. 204.

13. Ibid., p. 202.

14. Spencer Penrose, www.en.wikipedia.org/wiki/Spencer_Penrose.

15. J. Frank Wilson, M.D., and C. M. Chahbazian, M.D., "Penrose Cancer Hospital 1949–1974: A Quarter Century of Achievement—A Tribute to Juan A. del Regato, M.D.," *International Journal of Radiation Oncology, Biology and Physics,* v. 15, June 29, 1988, pp. 1475–1476.

16. Ibid., p. 1476.

17. Roger Robison Oral History Interview with Dr. Jacques Ovadia, Chicago, Illinois, September 11, 2002, p. 2; *See also* Roger F. Robison, "The Race for Megavoltage X-Rays Versus Telegamma," *Acta Oncologica,* vol. 34, no. 8, 1995.

18. David Larson Oral History Interview with Dr. David Castro, October 22, 2002, p. 2.

19. Roger Robison Oral History Interview with Dr. Jacques Ovadia, p. 2.

20. Ibid.

21. Juan del Regato, M.D., *A History of the Radiological Sciences*, "Gilbert Fletcher (1911–1992)," *See also* "Gilbert H. Fletcher, 81, Cancer Therapy Expert," *The New York Times,* January 13, 1992.

22. Juan del Regato, M.D., *A History of the Radiological Sciences*, "Henry S. Kaplan (1918–1984)," p. 246.

23. Ibid.

24. Ibid.

25. Malcolm A. Bagshaw, et al., "Memorial Resolution," p. 1.

26. Juan del Regato, M.D., *A History of the Radiological Sciences*, "Henry S. Kaplan (1918–1984)," p. 246.

27. Ibid.

28. David Hussey Tape-recorded Telephone Oral History Interview with Philip Rubin, Rochester, New York, October 7, 2003, p. 9.

29. Ibid., p. 1.

30. Ibid., p. 9.

31. Program for Henry Seymour Kaplan Memorial Service, Stanford University, February 12, 1984.

32. Luther Brady and David Hussey Tape-recorded Oral History Interview with Robert G. Parker, Chicago, Illinois, December 1, 2004, p. 11.

33. Ibid., p. 2.

34. Ibid.

Simeon T. Cantril, founding member and first president of the American Club of Therapeutic Radiologists.

CHAPTER FOUR

The American Club
of Therapeutic Radiologists

R obert G. Parker's introduction to the American Club of Therapeutic Radiologists (ACTR) was through his boss at the time, Simeon T. Cantril (1908–1959). Parker, who was then Cantril's junior associate in Seattle, recalled that Cantril flew home from the organizational meeting of the ACTR in Chicago and "informed me that I was a member of a newly formed medical society."[1]

Parker, who would serve a term as ASTRO's president seventeen years later, recalled being one of the founding members of the ACTR. He had joined Cantril and Franz Buschke (1902–1983), another founding member, at the Tumor Institute of the Swedish Hospital in Seattle in 1955. At the time, Cantril was one of the leading lights of American radiotherapy.[2]

Parker, who had trained under Isadore Lampe (1906–1982) at the University of Michigan, at the same time as Philip Rubin and Malcolm Bagshaw, had hoped to stay in Ann Arbor after his residency. But Lampe urged him to go elsewhere for a year, and then come back to Michigan. Parker recalled that Lampe suggested that "there are two people out in Seattle, Simeon Cantril and Franz Buschke. He said, 'If you want my advice, I would go to Seattle because there are two of them there, and one of them is always likely to be in town, and if you go to any of the other places, you're very likely to not see the man you're there to train with.'"[3]

Lampe was a giant in the field. Born in London in 1906, he went to medical school at Western Reserve University and trained in radiology. He spent his entire career on the faculty of the University of Michigan, and he taught radiotherapy to hundreds of residents.[4] Many of these later chaired academic departments or divisions, including Malcolm Bagshaw, Howard Latourette, Philip Rubin, Ray Ridings, Jose Campos, Bob Parker, Seymour Levitt, Juan Fayos, Pat Cavanaugh, and Ruheri Perez-Tamayo.

Parker took Lampe's advice and spent the year with Cantril and Buschke, but when it came time to return to Michigan, Cantril urged Parker to remain in Seattle. Parker, however, had promised Lampe he would return to the department at Michigan, so he called Lampe to tell him of the offer. "I am extremely proud that they think enough of you to want to keep you," Lampe told Parker.[5] Parker remembered thinking that "this is a man who had kept a faculty position open for one year for me, and that was his response. I can't imagine anyone being more graceful."[6]

The other thing that impressed Parker about his years with Cantril and Buschke in Seattle was just how few radiotherapists were in practice at the time. Shortly after taking the position at the University of Washington, Buschke left Seattle to head the Radiation Therapy Department at the University of California–San Francisco, and Cantril died of a sudden massive heart attack in 1959.

"I looked around and I was the only trained radiation oncologist in the states of Washington, Alaska, Montana, and Idaho," Parker said, "and now there are, I think, fourteen radiation oncologists at Swedish Hospital alone or something like that—another twelve at the university. That's sort of an interesting thing to happen during your lifetime, to see oncology develop in a part of the country where it didn't exist."[7]

Robert Parker, a club founder, was informed in 1958 by his boss, Simeon Cantril, that he would be joining ACTR. Parker served as president of ASTR in 1975–1976.

The First President, 1958–1959

Parker attributed the impetus for the growth of the specialty in the Pacific Northwest to Cantril, the first president of ACTR. Simeon Cantril was the son of a physician and a graduate of the Harvard University Medical School. Cantril had served his internship at the Mayo Clinic in Minnesota and later trained at Michael Reese Hospital in Chicago. While he was at Michael Reese, Cantril was befriended by Max Cutler, who urged Cantril to continue his studies in Europe. In 1935, he applied for and was accepted for training in therapeutic radiology at the Radium Institute of the University of Paris, which was chaired by Henri Coutard.[8]

At the time, Juan del Regato was in Paris as Coutard's assistant. "I initiated him in the routines of the department," del Regato said. "He stayed for two years before returning to the United States in 1937."[9]

Cantril, del Regato, Franz Buschke, Coutard, and Cutler joined the staff of the ill-fated Chicago Tumor Institute in 1938. They dispersed the following year when the Institute began having financial problems. Coutard went to Colorado Springs, Max Cutler to Beverly Hills, del Regato to Washington, DC, while Cantril and Buschke were recruited to the Tumor Institute of the Swedish Hospital in Seattle.

During World War II, Cantril served as a consultant to the US government's Manhattan Project.[10] In the years following the war, Cantril continued his consulting, primarily for the Atomic Energy Commission and for General Electric. In 1950, Cantril, Buschke, and physicist Herbert Parker, all of Seattle, published a book, *Supervoltage Roentgentherapy*, laying the framework for the advances in radiotherapy practice in the future with

Isadore Lampe, a club founder, taught radiation therapy to hundreds of residents at the University of Michigan.

Howard B. Latourette, one of the founding members of ACTR.

equipment operating at more than 500 kV.[11] Cantril's reputation and his extensive list of contacts within the field made him a natural for holding office in the ACTR.

Cantril immediately began to ensure that the club followed through on suggestions to have scientific sessions at the organization's semiannual meetings. When the ACTR met at the Homestead in Hot Springs, Virginia, on April 8, 1959, lunch was followed by a 12:30 p.m. symposium in the Homestead's Georgian Room on "The Training of Therapeutic Radiologists." Cantril introduced the subject and the presenters, who included Gilbert Fletcher, Henry Kaplan, Victor Marcial, Frank Batley, Robert Robbins, and Jerome Vaeth.[12]

Cantril was planning another scientific symposium for the ACTR's annual meeting in Chicago in November 1959 when he was stricken with a massive heart attack in Seattle on September 10, 1959. The club had lost one of its most illustrious members, and many of the founding members had lost an esteemed associate.

"Cantril was a quiet, reserved, keen observer," del Regato eulogized his longtime comrade. "He was hard working and methodical. He was also a sincere friend and a sensitive man. He was wholly devoted to the interests of American radiotherapy. He was the first American secretary of the International Club of Therapeutic Radiologists and was the Janeway Lecturer of the American Radium Society in 1956. He was also the first president of the ACTR.

"In Dr. Cantril, American radiotherapy lost one of its most valuable assets, and I personally lost my best friend."[13]

The Early Meetings

Simeon Cantril's untimely death in 1959 led to the appointment of J. W. J. Carpender of the University of Chicago to fill the unexpired portion of his term. Carpender served a term in his own right in 1959–1960. He was followed as president by Milton Friedman (1903–1983) in 1960–1961 and Manuel Garcia (1907–1973) in 1961–1962.

All three were radiotherapists of wide renown and scholarship. Carpender headed the radiation therapy section at the University of Chicago from 1948 until 1965 and also served as president of the American Board of Radiology and the Radiological Society of North America during his tenure.[14] He distinguished himself with his work on the use of radiation therapy for early stage laryngeal cancer.[15]

James W. J. Carpender, a founding member of the club, was named ACTR's second president when Simeon Cantril died in 1959.

Friedman, a native of Newark, New Jersey, was one of the first Americans to be certified in therapeutic radiology by the American Board of Radiology; that was in 1934. During World War II, he was given a commission in the US Army and assigned to head the Department of Radiotherapy at Walter Reed Hospital at Washington, DC.[16]

Following the war, Friedman was appointed head of the Department of Radiation Therapy of the New York University Hospital in New York City, where demand for radiation therapy services had spiked in the years after World War II. By 1951, Friedman and his associates at the cancer hospital were treating 1,555 new cases a year.[17] Long affiliated with the Oak Ridge Institute for Nuclear Studies (ORINS), Friedman, in collaboration with Marshall Brucer and Elizabeth Anderson, edited an influential transcript of a 1958 ORINS symposium on supervoltage radiation therapy.[18]

Manuel Garcia did pioneering work in treatment of cancer of the cervix at Charity Hospital in New Orleans. A native of Mexico, Garcia graduated from Tulane Medical School during the depths of the Great Depression and did his residency in radiology at Memorial Hospital in New York. It was at Memorial that Garcia began his lifelong study of radiotherapy, and when he returned to New Orleans in the early 1940s, Garcia accepted an appointment as assistant professor of radiology at Tulane, his alma mater. During the next thirty years, Garcia shaped radiotherapy education with his teaching at Tulane.[19]

Milton Friedman, one of the founders of ACTR and third president of the club, 1960–1961.

The ACTR's structure changed little during the presidencies of Carpender, Friedman, and Garcia. Dinner meetings were held in conjunction with the annual meeting of the RSNA during late November or early December, and luncheon meetings were held in the spring in conjunction with the annual meeting of the American Radium Society.

The scientific session that Cantril had established in 1959 continued. At the 1959 fall meeting in Chicago, Carpender organized a symposium to discuss the radiation therapy equipment needs for a hospital of seven hundred beds. Franz Buschke, Jesshill Love, Jean Bouchard, and Milford Schulz described their experience with hospitals in San Francisco, Dallas, Montreal, and Boston.[20]

The dinner meetings continued to be what del Regato described as "Dutch" affairs. Members paid no dues or convention fees, and they were expected to make their reservations with the secretary well in advance and pay for their meal at the door, in cash.

Manuel Garcia, a founding member of the club and fourth president of ACTR, 1961–1962.

J. Frank Wilson was one of the dozens of interns and residents whom del Regato brought to the RSNA meeting each fall during the late 1950s and 1960s. "At the time," he said, "Jim Cox and I were residents together. We went to the RSNA in Chicago in the fall of 1966. All sessions were plenary, and we met in the Red Lacquer Ballroom in the Palmer House. It was quite possible at that meeting to see every practicing radiation oncologist in the United States."[21]

One of the great thrills for Wilson at those early ACTR meetings was the opportunity of rubbing shoulders with the grand old men of radiation therapy. "During that first conference in 1966," he said, "I met Maurice Lenz and Isadore Lampe. They were all there, including Franz Buschke."[22]

Other elements of the annual meeting were less impressive. Wilson recalled that "the exhibit space, in retrospect, was laughable. There was no equipment, and there were only a few vendors' tables."[23]

Del Regato expected the residents to work for their admission. Most stayed in drafty dormitory-style rooms at the nearby University Club for $6 a day, their night's sleep interrupted by the racket of the passage of Chicago's elevated railway.[24]

Franz J. Buschke, one of the founders of ACTR and president of ASTR in 1963–1964.

For ACTR's annual dinner meeting, members couldn't get in the door of the banquet room without first settling accounts with del Regato's residents. "The Chief asked Jim Cox and myself to sell tickets at the door," Wilson explained of his first visit to an ACTR convention. "He was a stickler for making exact change. He would tell us, 'Don't let so and so get in without paying.' At one point, Jim and I were counting the money, and del Regato came out to check on things. He said we could eat if we would pay for our dinner. He then went around to give everybody their change, which was something like $1.32."[25] Cox was later the very successful treasurer of ASTRO.

Membership Requirements

Membership criteria continued to draw substantial discussion during ACTR's early years. The founding members were sticklers for limiting membership to physicians who practiced radiotherapy exclusively. As early as November 1959, the membership committee rejected a Portland, Oregon candidate when he admitted that approximately 20 percent of his caseload was diagnostic radiology.[26]

At that same meeting, one of the founding members, Sidney Rubenfeld of New York City, raised the question of the amount of diagnostic radiology in his own practice. Rubenfeld noted that 10 percent of his practice had always consisted of radiodiagnosis, although he had considered the diagnostic work to be ancillary to his radiotherapy practice.

But, Rubenfeld noted, the diagnostic component had now increased to about 25 percent of his practice. Rubenfeld added that since others were being refused membership for similar work loads, he felt he would not be eligible for membership on the same basis.[27] The ACTR's Executive Committee elected not to take action, but did note that the Founders Agreement contained a proviso whereby a member should resign if he no longer complied with the club's membership requirements. Milton Friedman offered to talk the matter over privately with Rubenfeld when he returned to New York City.

Rubenfeld's honesty was evident just one month later when he wrote a letter of resignation to the club secretary.[28] Rubenfeld's dilemma was not unknown at the time, especially among ACTR members in private practice. Reading X-rays one or two days a week sometimes meant the difference between a profitable and nonprofitable practice for a radiotherapist in the late 1950s and early 1960s. Rubenfeld was simply expressing a reality that more than one radiotherapist had to deal with during the period.

Del Regato and the founders were adamant that the ACTR should be open only to radiologist opportunities practicing straight radiotherapy. The founders felt that diagnostic radiologists had sufficient outlets for research and education, while the radiotherapist opportunities were more limited. Rubenfeld's resignation was accepted, and the Executive Committee urged amending the Founders Agreement to require sponsorship of every new member by two existing members who would submit the prospective

The Founding Members

When the steering committee of the American Club of Therapeutic Radiologists met at the Shoreham Hotel in Washington, DC, on October 1, 1958, the primary order of business was approving the American club's founding members. A total of eighty radiotherapists from across the United States had submitted applications for membership in the new organization. One was rejected because of the amount of time he spent in diagnostic radiology.

The first seventy-nine members accepted were:

J. R. Andrews	Bethesda, Maryland	Howard B. Latourette	Ann Arbor, Michigan
Colonel Harry L. Berman	Washington, D.C.	Maurice Lenz	New York, New York
Robert J. Bloor	Detroit, Michigan	Leonard M. Liegner	New York, New York
Fernando J. Bloedorn	Baltimore, Maryland	R. Kenneth Loeffler	Madison, Wisconsin
Charles M. Botstein	New York, New York	Jesshill Love	Louisville, Kentucky
J. Ernest Breed	Chicago, Illinois	John T. Mallams	Dallas, Texas
Harry W. Burnett Jr.	New York, New York	Victor A. Marcial	Rio Piedras, Puerto Rico
J. Franz Buschke	San Francisco, California	Charles L. Martin	Dallas, Texas
Simeon T. Cantril	Seattle, Washington	Esther C. Marting	Cincinnati, Ohio
J. W. J. Carpender	Chicago, Illinois	Lowell S. Miller	Houston, Texas
James T. Case	Santa Barbara, California	William T. Moss	Chicago, Illinois
Ralph M. Caulk	Washington, DC	Donn Mosser	Minneapolis, Minnesota
Patrick J. Cavanaugh	Louisville, Kentucky	Walter T. Murphy	Buffalo, New York
Chu H. Chang	New Haven, Connecticut	James J. Nickson	New York, New York
Donald S. Childs Jr.	Rochester, Minnesota	Robert G. Parker	Seattle, Washington
Florence Chu	New York, New York	Harold Perry	Cincinnati, Ohio
Joseph Concannon	Philadelphia, Pennsylvania	Bryan L. Redd	Atlanta, Georgia
Carlo A. Cuccia	Baltimore, Maryland	Juan A. del Regato	Colorado Springs, Colorado
Robert J. Dickson	Baltimore, Maryland	Robert Robbins	Philadelphia, Pennsylvania
Theodore P. Eberhard	Ann Arbor, Michigan	Rieva Rosh	New York, New York
John C. Evans	New York, New York	Bernard Roswit	New York, New York
Wesley G. Farnsley	Louisville, Kentucky	Sidney Rubenfeld	New York, New York
Gilbert H. Fletcher	Houston, Texas	Philip Rubin	Rochester, New York
Robert E. Fricke	Rochester, Minnesota	P. Scanlon	Rochester, Minnesota
Jacob R. Fried	New York, New York	Martin Schneider	Galveston, Texas
Miltion Friedman	New York, New York	Milford D. Shulz	Boston, Massachusetts
Manuel Garcia	New Orleans, Louisiana	Gleen E. Sheline	San Francisco, California
David C. Gastineau	Indianapolis, Indiana	Sidney M. Silverstone	New York, New York
M. Greenberg	Milwaukee, Wisconsin	Martha E. Southard	Philadelphia, Pennsylvania
R. J. Guttman	New York, New York	Justin J. Stein	Los Angeles, California
Anna Hamann	Chicago, Illinois	J. P. Storaasli	Cleveland, Ohio
Irvin F. Hummon Jr.	Chicago, Illinois	Herman D. Suit	Bethesda, Maryland
Harold W. Jacox	New York, New York	Norah D. Tapley	New York, New York
H. L. Jaffe	Los Angeles California	Erich M. Uhlmann	Chicago, Illinois
Erwin M. Japha	Glencoe, Illinois	Jerome M. Vaeth	San Francisco, California
Henry S. Kaplan	San Francisco, California	Martin Van Herik	Rochester, Minnesota
Morton Kligerman	New Haven, Connecticut	Halvor Vermund	Madison, Wisconsin
K. L. Krabbenhoft	Detroit, Michigan	Orliss Wildermuth	Seattle, Washington
Simon Kramer	Philadelphia, Pennsylvania	T. H. S. Wolever	Houston, Texas
Isadore Lampe	Ann Arbor, Michigan		

Anna Hamann, a founding member of ACTR.

Charles Martin, one of the founders of ACTR.

Fernando Bloedorn, a founding member of ACTR.

Florence Chu, one of the founding members of the club.

Harold Jacox, another of the ACTR founding members.

Morton M. Kligerman, a founder of ACTR.

Lillian M. Fuller, a founding member of ACTR.

Ralph M. Scott, one of the founders of ACTR.

    The list of founding members was not closed, however, until the day following the founders meeting. The Membership Committee, consisting of Simeon Cantril, J. W. J. Carpender, and Juan A. del Regato met at the Palmer House on Wednesday, November 19, 1958, to approve nineteen additional founding members, whose applications had arrived after the Steering Committee meeting on October 1. The additional nineteen members were:

Malcolm Bagshaw	San Francisco, California	John R. McLaren	Atlanta, Georgia
Ernest J. Braun	Houston, Texas	Paul M. Meadows	Pittsburgh, Pennsylvania
Blaine R. Brown	Salt Lake City, Utah	Raul Mercado	Baltimore, Maryland
Frank V. Comas	Oak Ridge, Tennessee	Frederick W. O'Brien Jr.	Cleveland, Ohio
Lillian M. Fuller	Houston, Texas	Thomas C. Pomeroy	Columbus, Ohio
Melvin L. Griem	Chicago, Illinois	Jose M. Sala	Columbia, Missouri
Jose R. Herrera Jr.	Houston, Texas	Martha C. Schmidt	Buffalo, New York
Melville L. Jacobs	Arcadia, Illinois	Ralph M. Scott	Sayre, Pennsylvania
Robert E. Lee	Rochester, Minnesota	Emanuel G. Tulsky	Philadelphia, Pennsylvania
David J. Lochman	Chicago, Illinois		

The addition of nineteen radiotherapists brought the American Club's founding membership to ninety-eight people.

member's candidacy to the entire membership for approval. The Executive Committee also urged reducing the number of necessary unfavorable veto votes from ten to five.[29] These changes were unanimously approved at the membership meeting on March 18, 1960.[30]

The Original 111 Members

In 1958–1959, its first full year of operation, the American Club of Therapeutic Radiologists surveyed its membership and printed a demographic portrait of ACTR's members. At the time, there were 111 members practicing in twenty-four states, the District of Columbia, and the Commonwealth of Puerto Rico.

The greatest number of members was from New York, California, and Illinois. Forty-five of the members lived and worked in these three states, half of them in New York. A total of eighty-seven members were graduates of American medical schools, while twenty-four members had earned their degrees from foreign medical schools. Harvard Medical School had the largest representation with six graduates, followed by Northwestern University Medical School with five.[31]

Most of the members were forty to fifty-five years old, about 20 percent of were still in their twenties and thirties, and an equal percentage of members were over fifty-five.[32] James T. Case of California was the oldest member, at seventy-eight, and Robert E. Fricke had been practicing radiotherapy since 1920. Of the first 111 members, 20 had taken their entire specialty training outside the United States. The vast majority—104 members—were diplomates of the American Board of Radiology, 41 in therapeutic radiology exclusively.[33]

Three-quarters of the membership had full-time institutional affiliation, and another twenty-four members had part-time institutional affiliation. Only six members engaged solely in the private practice of radiotherapy. Some seventy-four of the institutional members held a medical school appointment, twenty-two as full professors of radiology (including three emeritus appointments and two department chairmen), twenty-three associate professors, twenty assistant professors and nine instructors. More than two-thirds of the ACTR's membership was engaged in some aspect of radiotherapy research.[34]

A total of thirty members were fellows of the American College of Radiology; sixty-five members belonged to RSNA, and sixty-three were members of the Radium Society; thirty-seven were members of the American Roentgen Ray Society; twenty-eight members belonged to the Society for Nuclear Medicine; twelve members also were members of the Society of University Radiologists, and seven belonged to the Radiation Research Society. In 1959, only ten club members were women, four members were Canadians, and one was Cuban.[35]

Simeon Cantril was the first of the founding members to die, in September 1959. Two other founding members followed him within a year. James T. Case (1882–1960) died in Santa Barbara, California, in

James T. Case, one of the founding member of ACTR in 1958.

May 1960. Case was a 1905 graduate of the Seventh-Day Adventist American Missionary (medical) College of Battle Creek in Chicago. Case did pioneering work in radiotherapy with the first Coolidge 200-kV deep therapy tube (1922) while working for John Kellogg at the famous Battle Creek Sanitarium.[36] His later career in Chicago was primarily devoted to diagnostic radiology. He was a professor at Northwestern University from 1913 to 1947. He moved to California in 1955, where he devoted his time to directing the Department of Radiotherapy in the Cancer Foundation at Santa Barbara's Cottage Hospital. At the time, Case was the only American radiologist who had been invited to give the Caldwell, Carman, and Janeway Lectures.[37]

Case's death in 1960 was followed in August 1960 by the death of Theodore Eberhard, del Regato's predecessor at the Ellis Fischel Cancer Hospital. Following World War II service in New Caledonia, Eberhard had organized the Department of Radiotherapy at the Jefferson Medical College in Philadelphia.

The "Young Turks"

Already by the early 1960s, the Executive Committee was recruiting new blood for membership in the American Club of Therapeutic Radiologists. And some of those new members quickly began to advocate the establishment of a more formal organization to represent members in the growing field.

A third-generation Texan and graduate of the Baylor Medical School, Herman D. Suit was just back from studies at Oxford in the late 1950s when the ACTR was being formed. A founding member of the club, Suit was at the National Cancer Institute in Bethesda, Maryland, at the time of the club's first meetings. What he and some of the younger members experienced during those meetings in the late 1950s left something to be desired. Suit had done radiation related scientific research in Oxford for almost three-and-a-half years and had a novel understanding of the scientific prestige radiation oncology enjoyed in Europe.

"The radiotherapy component was always at the tail end of everything," Suit recalled of the ACTR meetings at RSNA in Chicago. "The meeting room was always next to the kitchen, and we had to put up with the clattering of dishes. The club always had to meet in the second or third basement. In terms of a professional sense, it was third-rate. I had come from England where radiology and radiotherapy were treated very well. Professionally, there was no ambience."[38]

Suit began meeting with other young founding members of ACTR, including Malcolm Bagshaw, Melvin Griem, and William Powers. They typically scheduled a luncheon meeting during the week of the RSNA meetings in Chicago. Malcolm Bagshaw was a member of the faculty at Stanford. Griem was the longtime director of the Department of Radiation Therapy at the University of Chicago, and Powers was then head of the Radiotherapy Division at the Mallinckrodt Institute of Radiology at

Herman D. Suit, one of ASTR's "Young Turks," was president of ASTRO in 1980–1981.

William E. Powers, another of the club's "Young Turks," and president of ASTR in 1970–1971.

The Crab

For much of its early history, ASTRO and its predecessor, the American Club of Therapeutic Radiologists (ACTR), were represented by a logo that depicted a crab against a background of the interlocking rings of the atomic symbol.

The crab–signifying cancer–and the atomic symbol were favorites of Juan del Regato, the club's first executive secretary. Del Regato designed the logo for the club and had an artist in Colorado Springs execute the design into a logo suitable for use on ACTR letterheads. Later, after he incorporated the *club* as a *society* in 1962, del Regato had the design changed slightly to incorporate the words "American Society for Therapeutic Radiology and Oncology" into the ring encircling the crab and atomic symbol.[1]

"I remember del Regato showing us the design for the crab logo," said J. Frank Wilson, who served a residency under del Regato at Penrose Cancer Hospital in Colorado Springs in 1966. "He personally generated a lot of ASTRO paraphernalia."[2]

The 1958 logo of the American Club of Therapeutic Radiologists.

When Penrose dedicated its new Cancer Hospital Research Building in 1970, del Regato contributed a variation of the crab design for the Colorado hospital's logo.[3] This time, the crab sprawled atop a globe, with parts of North America and the bulge of Africa gripped in its claws.[4]

Endnotes

1. Raymond A. Gagliardi and J. Frank Wilson, *A History of the Radiological Sciences: Radiation Oncology* (Reston, Virginia: Radiology Centennial, Inc., 1996), p. 178.

2. Bill Beck Interview with J. Frank Wilson, p. 3.

3. "Dedication and Blessing of the Penrose Cancer Hospital Research Building," Sunday, December 6, 1970, p. 4.

4. J. Frank Wilson, *Penrose Cancer Hospital, 1949-1974: A Quarter Century of Achievement–A Tribute to Juan A. del Regato, M.D.*, p. 1482.

Washington University in St. Louis. These three took active leadership roles with ACTR in the 1970s.

"We were the Young Turks," Suit explained. "We all pushed for scientific programs, and our proposals were met with a negative response. The Executive Committee said that the radiologists would cut us out completely. We replied that we're already cut out. We went to a couple of the senior guys and told them we'd rather form our own society. We were determined that existing arrangements were no longer viable."[39] Suit and the Young Turks were articulating a feeling that the specialty had evolved to the point where it needed its own identity that would include separate research and educational sessions at the annual meeting, a paid staff, and an independent, peer-reviewed journal.

In the mid-1960s, Suit and the Young Turks forced the issue. "We sent a letter to the president of the club, cosigned by Mal Bagshaw, Bill Powers, and myself. We sent it to Milford Schulz, the president of the club. He was one of the first people in the United States to work with supervoltage, at the Collis P. Huntington Hospital in Boston in 1937. He then went to Massachusetts General Hospital."[40]

Suit called the letter "a very polite, but unambiguous request."[41] It essentially urged ACTR to transform itself into a full-fledged society, which the club was already in the process of doing.

"We all felt that we had a role in the transformation from a club to a society," Suit said. That transformation took place in the early 1960s, and it positioned ACTR for the rapid growth in the practice of radiotherapy that took place throughout the decade.

Melvin Griem, one of ASTR's "Young Turks."

Malcolm A. Bagshaw, another of the "Young Turks," was president of ASTR in 1972-1973.

Endnotes

1. Letter from Robert G. Parker to Martin Coleman, Chair of ASTRO History Committee, June 13, 2003, p. 1.

2. Ibid., p. 2.

3. Luther Brady and David Hussey Tape-recorded Oral History Interview with Robert G. Parker, Chicago, Illinois, December 1, 2004, p. 5.

4. Juan A. del Regato, *Radiological Oncologists: The Unfolding of a Medical Specialty*, pp.187–195.

5. Ibid., pp. 5–6.

6. Ibid., p. 6.

7. Ibid., p. 7.

8. *Record of Proceedings, American Club of Therapeutic Radiologists*, September 10, 1959, p. 12.

9. Ibid.

10. Leon O. Jacobson, "From Atom to Eve," *Perspectives in Biology and Medicine*, vol. 24, no. 2, Winter 1981, p. 203.

11. Juan A. del Regato, "100 Years of Radiation Oncology," in *Current Radiation Oncology*, Jeffrey S. Tobias, ed., v. 2 (Oxford: Oxford University Press, 1986), p. 24; *See also* Roger F. Robison, "The Race for Megavoltage X-Rays Versus Telegamma," *Acta Oncologica*, vol. 34, no. 8, 1995.

12. *Record of Proceedings, American Club of Therapeutic Radiologists*, September 10, 1959, p. 9.

13. Ibid.

14. *The University of Chicago, Department of Radiology, History*, "Radiation Therapy," http://www.radiology.uchicago.edu/radtherapy.htm.

15. "News Item," *CA-Bulletin of Cancer Progress*, vol. 10, no. 5, September–October 1960, p. 178.

16. Juan A. del Regato, *Radiological Oncologists: The Unfolding of a Medical Specialty* (Reston, Virginia: Radiology Centennial, Inc., 1993), p. 239.

17. Nancy Knight, "Training and Education," *Radiation Oncology*, p. 181.

18. E. R. N. Grigg, *The Trail of the Invisible Light from X-Strahlen to Radio(bio)logy*, pp. 298–299.

19. Juan A. del Regato, *Radiological Oncologists: The Unfolding of a Medical Specialty*, p. 240.

20. *Record of Proceedings, American Club of Therapeutic Radiologists*, November 17, 1959, p. 15.

21. Bill Beck Interview with J. Frank Wilson, p. 2.

22. Ibid.

23. Ibid.

24. Ibid.

25. Ibid.

26. *Record of Proceedings, American Club of Therapeutic Radiologists*, November 17, 1959, p. 15.

27. Ibid., p. 13.

28. *Record of Proceedings, American Club of Therapeutic Radiologists*, March 16, 1960, p. 17.

29. Ibid.

30. *Record of Proceedings, American Club of Therapeutic Radiologists*, March 18, 1960, p. 19.

31. "Ionized Minutiae," *ACTR Directory*, 1959.

32. Ibid.

33. Ibid.

34. Ibid.

35. Ibid.

36. Roger F. Robison, "The Race for Megavoltage X-Rays Versus Telegamma," *Acta Oncologica*, vol. 34, no. 8, 1995, p. 1061.

37. *Record of Proceedings, American Club of Therapeutic Radiologists*, May 22, 1960.

38. Bill Beck Tape-recorded Oral History Interview with Herman D. Suit, Philadelphia, Pennsylvania, November 4, 2006, p. 2.

39. Ibid., pp. 2–3.

40. Ibid., p. 3; *See also* Roger F. Robison, "The Race for Megavoltage X-Rays Versus Telegamma," *Acta Oncologica*, vol. 34, no. 8, 1995, p. 1064. One of Schulz's colleagues was the first radiotherapist to treat a patient, a dentist with bladder cancer, with a true 1 mV (constant potential) therapy beam, in 1937. The patient outlived the hospital, which closed in 1941.

41. Ibid.

Milford Schulz, ACTR president in 1964–1965,
chaired an ad hoc committee that recommended the
transition from a club to a professional society.

CHAPTER FIVE

The American Society of Therapeutic Radiologists

or ASTRO, the 1960s were an era of sometime slow growth punctuated by momentous changes, both for the organization and the practice of medicine in the United States. ASTRO began the decade as "the club," a chapter of the International Club of Radiotherapists. It ended the 1960s as a full-fledged society, the American Society of Therapeutic Radiologists (ASTR), a name adopted in 1966.

Renaming the Club in 1966

By 1966, radiation therapy, like all specialties, was facing significant changes in how medicine was practiced in the United States. President Lyndon B. Johnson had made healthcare a cornerstone of his Great Society. In 1965, Congress passed and President Johnson signed the Medicare and Medicaid legislation that would transform the delivery of healthcare in the United States. The ink was hardly dry on the Medicare legislation when the American Club of Therapeutic Radiologists (ACTR) confronted the issue that had bedeviled the membership since the earliest meetings at Barney's Market Club in Chicago. Juan del Regato had pushed for the designation of a club rather than a society, mostly because of the small numbers of radiotherapists practicing in the United States during the 1950s. He had argued eloquently and forcefully that the club's founding as a chapter of the International Club of Radiotherapists would give members the freedom to organize their affairs without interference from the larger societies that at the time catered primarily to the diagnostic radiology community.

What complicated the discussion for radiotherapists was the simple fact that in the 1950s and for most of the 1960s, the lion's share of radiotherapy treatments were delivered by general radiologists. In fact, the numbers treated by physicians trained in general radiology dwarfed the number treated by specialists trained in straight radiotherapy. In academic centers, there was a de facto sub-specialization, i.e., radiation therapy being performed by radiologists who confined their practice to radiation therapy.

By 1966, the American Club of Therapeutic Radiologists had been in existence for almost ten years. During that time, the organization had grown from an original membership of just 98 to an organization of 250 members. The growth had occurred concurrently with the growth and recognition of radiotherapy as a medical specialty in the United States. Members were understandably proud of the role that the club had played during those years, but now that the membership had grown larger, most of the leaders felt that it was time to formalize the structure of the organization.

At an Executive Committee meeting held on April 14, 1966, the ad hoc Committee on Organization, composed of Milford Schulz, Malcolm Bagshaw, William Powers, Juan del Regato, and Herman Suit, issued a report on why the ACTR should move to formalize its organizational structure. The Committee wanted the club to assume the various responsibilities and functions of a professional society.[1]

The members of the ad hoc committee judged that a more formal organization could better serve the needs and interests of radiotherapy, in general. In a sense, the club had represented only a limited group, those who had trained in straight radiotherapy and a few members who had trained in general radiology but were well known as academic radiation therapists. Committee members noted that a formal society could more effectively represent radiotherapy to the community of general radiologists. It also could provide a convenient and respectable framework in which therapeutic radiology's maturation as a medical specialty could more easily continue. Society status would provide a focus of cohesion and sense of identity for the rapidly increasing number of radiation therapists, and it could serve as a forum for the interchange of ideas. It also would provide a place where interested groups could come for advice on matters related to radiotherapy. Finally, a formal society would encourage research in radiation therapy and provide a forum for presenting that research at the society's annual meetings.[2]

At a luncheon meeting the following day, the proposal of forming a specialty society was turned over to the membership for discussion. As at the time of the founding of the American Club in 1958, some doctors cautioned against proceeding too rapidly with formalization. Others in the room argued that there was a need for radiotherapists and medical physicists to have their own organization that could better represent their interests, promote research, and provide better education.[3]

After further debate, the proposal was put to a mail ballot vote, the measure passed overwhelmingly that spring of 1966, and the ACTR became the American Society of Therapeutic Radiologists (ASTR). Also passing handily were proposals to create the status of Associate Member for such specialists as radiobiologists, radiation physicists, nuclear medicine specialists, and tumor pathologists. And a Corresponding Membership category was created for therapeutic radiologists living and practicing in Canada, Latin America, and other parts of the world.

ASTR was now ready to assume the responsibilities and functions of a professional society that would further the education of its members and the promotion of radiotherapy as a medical specialty.

Creation of the Board of Directors

Transition from a club to a society required some changes in governance. Initially, when the American Club was founded in 1958, the Executive Committee was comprised of the president, vice-president, and secretary. A treasurer was added when the club started assessing membership dues in 1962, but the treasurer didn't become part of the Executive Committee until 1965.

That same year, at an Executive Committee meeting held on November 28, 1965, James Nickson, the president at the time, put forth a proposal to enlarge the membership of the Executive Committee to seven members by adding the immediate past-president and two members elected at-large from the general membership of the organization.[4] The motion was approved by the general membership at the next meeting in Phoenix, Arizona, on April 15, 1966. Henceforth, the Executive Committee would be composed of the president, vice-president, secretary, treasurer, the immediate past-president and the two members elected at-large elected from the general membership.[5]

Another proposal that the membership of the ACTR approved in a May 1966 mail ballot changed the name of the Executive Committee to that

And It Was Very Informal

One of the more pleasant memories of the club for longtime members is the camaraderie that was involved in the early days. Theodore Brickner joined the American Society for Therapeutic Radiologists (ASTR) during his residency in the early 1960s, when it was still officially "the club."

"When I was in residency," Brickner recalled, "there was the American Club of Therapeutic Radiologists. And del Regato, Fletcher, Brady, and others had built this little club, and they invited their residents and their ex-residents to participate. Once a year we all got together."

Brickner recalled attending the society's first scientific meetings in Phoenix. "Some of our meetings, we'd sit out on the grass at the hotel and have a meeting," he said. "And it was very informal. It was wonderful because you'd sit around, eight or ten or twelve people with somebody like Fletcher or del Regato, and talk to them about how did they do things. You learned so much. And people would come by, or somebody would come and say, 'Hey, here's what we've been doing,' and a new idea would be fleshed out. Everybody would sit around talking about it.

"Well, that got bigger and bigger and they eventually decided to make the club into a society. And there were a tremendous amount of politics involved."[1]

J. Frank Wilson recalled the give-and-take of those early meetings. He attended his first club meeting in 1966 in Chicago as a resident from Penrose Hospital in Colorado Springs and was astounded that he could rub shoulders with the giants in the field. Later, Wilson would attend the society's early scientific meetings at the Biltmore in Phoenix.

"I went from Penrose to the National Institutes of Health (NIH)," Wilson said. "I went to the first separate scientific meeting at the Biltmore in Phoenix. All of the sessions were plenary, with lots of discussion after every presentation. It was a better format than the format we have today, with very competitive personalities who would play to the audience."[2]

The informality that Brickner and Wilson recalled as residents during the days of the American Club carried over into the American Society. One of the highlights of the Biltmore scientific session was the afternoon-long luncheon and cocktail party on the lawn of the Arizona resort.

Endnotes

1. Dr. Paul Wallner Tape-recorded Oral History Interview with Dr. Theodore J. Brickner Jr., Tulsa, Oklahoma, n.d., p. 13.

2. Bill Beck Interview with J. Frank Wilson, p. 3.

of "Board of Directors." The measure passed overwhelmingly and gave indication that the club was quickly moving toward a more formal type of organization. Supporters of the proposal noted that the infrastructure was in place to enable the club to expand in an orderly manner and present itself as the principal society for the promotion of radiation therapy and the continuing education of radiation oncologists in the United States.

The transition to a formal society in 1966 put ASTR at the forefront of the forces marshaling to fight cancer, then as now, a disease that takes hundreds of thousands of lives each year.

Expanding the Research Base

The 1960s was an exciting era for the practice of radiation therapy. New breakthroughs in treatment and equipment were being introduced every year, and it began to appear that radiotherapy would play a growing role in the ongoing battle against cancer.

Cancer research blossomed in the 1960s with the establishment of research programs at major universities, national efforts to define a research program for the specialty and the establishment of cooperative clinical research, including programs in radiation biology, physics, technological improvements in equipment and chemotherapeutic agents. Chemotherapy came into its own during the 1960s and established medical oncology as a specialty field.

CRTS

Radiotherapy leaders in the 1960s were also interested in developing research and cooperative studies in radiation oncology and radiation physics. This was a period when a lot of cooperative groups were being formed. The emphasis on research resulted in a series of conferences, the first of which was held in Highland Park, Illinois, in 1959, and the second of which was held in May 1960 in Carmel, California. The result of these and many other subsequent meetings provided the catalyst for rapid exchange of information regarding treatment protocols and clinical trials. This need for collective reporting led to NCI's creation of the Committee for Radiation Therapy Studies (CRTS).

In order to advise the director of the National Cancer Institute on appropriate studies and research initiatives in radiation oncology, the Committee for Radiation Therapy Studies was formed at the suggestion of Kenneth Endicott, director of the National Cancer Institute. The first chairman of the committee was Gilbert Fletcher. With the cooperation of the outstanding leaders in radiation oncology, this committee galvanized the field of radiation oncology.[6] The CRTS, which later became the Committee for Radiation Oncology Studies (CROS), was first chaired by Gilbert Fletcher, then Simon Kramer and William E. Powers.[7]

During this period it was funded by the National Cancer Institute. When the CROS lost its NCI funding in 1982, it was reformed as the InterSociety Council for Radiation Oncology (ISCRO) through a joint cooperative effort

Two presidents of ASTR in the early 1970s: Simon Kramer, 1969–1970, and Luther W. Brady, 1971–1972.

among the national radiation oncology societies. And Luther Brady became the chairman when it was reconstituted as ISCRO. The Council included the American Association of Physicists in Medicine (AAPM) and the Radiation Research Society (RRS) with equal representation.

With the formation of the CRTS, later the CROS, then ISCRO, the radiation oncology community began functioning in a positive, coherent, cooperative way to maximize the potential for research in radiation therapy. Fletcher, Kramer, and Powers showed the way by serving as chairmen of an organization that led the way in the gathering and dissemination of information that would further the cause of radiation therapy and its continuing improvement.[8] The CRTS set the standards for clinical practice which were ultimately identified and documented by Simon Kramer, and later Gerald Hanks, through the Patterns of Care Studies (PCS).

The CRTS proposed and developed the "blue books" setting the standards for radiation therapy practice in terms of resources, facilities, and personnel. They were first published in 1972 and then revised in 1981, 1986, and 1991. The CRTS also developed and published the *Radiation Research Plans for Radiation Oncology* first in 1976, edited by Simon Kramer, with subsequent updates in 1979, 1982, and 1987 edited by Luther Brady, et al.[9]

RTOG

The CRTS also was responsible for the creation of the Radiation Therapy Oncology Group (RTOG), in 1968. The first chairman of the RTOG was Simon Kramer.[10]

One of those who worked closely with Kramer was Philip Rubin. He recalled that Fletcher at first was skeptical about the prospects for the RTOG. Rubin recalled Fletcher telling him that radiation therapy already had "too many cooperative groups. It's going to be tough to get another group going."[11]

Rubin took the constitution of the Eastern Cooperative Oncology Group (ECOG) and created a similar document for the RTOG. "I came back with it," Rubin said, "and Gilbert said it was a good idea. Simon and I talked. Simon was heir apparent to Gilbert's position, so he was going to move up. But because no new money was available, Simon and I founded the RTOG. Simon had the NCI money for the methotrexate clinical trial, and so I gave them the constitution I had written, and we went on and developed it."[12]

For Ted Phillips, "the Radiation Therapy Oncology Group has been extremely important to the specialty. There are a lot of important trials that come out every year from RTOG. It is extremely successful. It was a pleasure and an honor to participate in RTOG. I was head of the chemical modifiers committee and then became vice-chair for modalities and then later vice chair for the site oriented studies."[13]

The RTOG was formed by the CRTS in 1968, and it was funded by the National Cancer Institute in 1971. John Curry, later the executive director of the American College of Radiology (ACR), was Simon Kramer's department administrator at Jefferson in Philadelphia when Kramer was named chair of RTOG. Curry would be instrumental in providing administrative support to RTOG during the 1970s and 1980s. RTOG has had and continues to have a major role in coordinating the clinical, biological, and physics research efforts in radiation therapy. Since 1978, more than fifty thousand patients have been entered on more than 369 RTOG protocols. RTOG has continued to develop new protocols to cancer treatment by radiation therapy and other treatment modalities.[14] RTOG has resulted in significant improvements not only in local and regional control, but it has also positively affected survival. The RTOG also has confirmed the potential for organ preservation by using conservation surgery and radiation therapy.[15]

Education and Training

The American Club of Therapeutic Radiologists was interested in education from the very beginning, and members of the organization frequently engaged in a lively debate on how best to educate future radiotherapists. At the time, most of the residency training programs were in general radiology; very few institutions had programs exclusively devoted to training residents in straight radiotherapy.

At the annual meeting on December 7, 1960, Milton Friedman organized the scientific program, and he asked the membership to identify important factors for training radiotherapists. In particular, the survey asked whether surgery, pathology, physics, and radiobiology should be included as part of the curriculum. All in attendance agreed that they were an essential part of the training.[16]

Younger members pushed ASTR to improve the state of education and training. Herman Suit and Malcolm Bagshaw wrote a letter to Milford Schulz that they presented at the annual meeting on December 2, 1965. In the letter, Suit and Bagshaw requested that "there be a discussion of the type of radiotherapy organization in this country that would maximally expedite the development of radiotherapy in terms of: 1) standards of clinical practice; 2) teaching and training in radiotherapy; and 3) clinical and basic research."[17]

With the transformation of the organization from a club to a society, the issue of resident training gained real impetus. By 1968, there were fifty-nine institutions offering training in straight radiotherapy, where there had only been fifteen in 1960. There were ninety-two residents in training in straight radiotherapy in 1968, up nearly fourfold from twenty-six in 1960.[18]

Another concern the club dealt with at the time was medical school education. At the annual meeting on November 18, 1963, Simon Kramer followed up Friedman's work with the results of a survey that he had sent out to 102 medical schools. Kramer's survey showed that instruction in radiation therapy was mostly ignored in the first two years of a medical student's training and given to only about half of them in the third and fourth year, a percentage that remained remarkably constant for the next four decades. Electives in radiation therapy were available only one-third of the time in the third and fourth years.[19] More than half of the institutions considered their formal teaching in radiation therapy to be inadequate. The results of Kramer's survey presented a serious challenge to ASTR for upgrading the training and education of medical students and young radiotherapists.

The bylaws put into effect on July 1, 1968, provided for a Committee on Education and Training, which was to "concern itself with all matters pertaining to academic radiotherapy, standards of training, accreditation, and certification. It was to study all possible means of improvement in the medical school teaching of radiotherapy and cancer, in the organization of programs of training for radiotherapists, and in the curricula of radiotherapeutic technologists, etc."[20]

The new bylaws clearly established that ASTR considered resident and medical student education to be an important part of its mission.

United States Residents

Prior to the 1960s, the majority of radiotherapists in the United States had received at least part of their training at medical schools in Europe. This was due to the dearth of programs available at American universities.

Eleanor Montague was one of the earliest Americans to do a residency in radiotherapy in the United States. The Korean War was winding down in

Eleanor D. Montague, pioneer in breast cancer therapy.

1953 when she enrolled in a residency program at Columbia University. "So after nine months of pathology," she told an interviewer in 2003, "I went to Columbia and started the radiology residency, which at that time was two-and-a-third years of diagnostic and then nine months of radiotherapy. The diagnostic part of the residency was exciting and taught by a good staff, but the radiotherapy part was really fascinating. The professor at that time was Morton M. Kligerman."[21]

At the yearly meeting in December, Juan del Regato reported on a survey conducted in August of 1960. He had polled sixty-six different institutions throughout the United States as to the number of trainees in straight radiotherapy. Only fifteen institutions had residents in training in straight radiotherapy. There were a total of only twenty-six such residents in training in the United States mainland, plus five in Puerto Rico. There were only six hospitals in the country that had more than one resident in training, with Penrose Cancer Hospital having six, the Tumor Institute of Seattle with three, and four other hospitals with two each. Twelve other institutions had only one trainee apiece.[22]

Morton Kligerman, president of ASTR in 1968–1969.

Another concern was attracting residents to the field of radiation oncology. This was discussed at a 1959 meeting of the American Club of Therapeutic Radiologists. J. Franz Buschke spoke about the numerous difficulties encountered for the training of radiotherapists in university departments of radiology. He remarked that in his department at the University of Washington, special three-month fellowships for summer work were being offered to medical students in the hope that they might choose radiotherapy as their specialty.

Del Regato pointed out that various opportunities for training were not due to the size of the institution but to their ideological approach. He noted that "so long as the departments of radiology were planned without examining rooms, organized without regard to follow-up and residents were not taught to examine patients or prescribe radiation therapy and had no rights to hospitalization, such departments would find it very hard to attract candidates for training."[23]

By 1966, eight years after the formation of the American Club of Therapeutic Radiologists, the membership had grown to 250, a measure of the society's success in promoting radiotherapy residency and medical school training. Along with this growth came the expansion and recognition of radiotherapy as a medical specialty in the United States. In the coming years, the organization would succeed in effectively representing radiotherapy to the community of general radiologists, the medical community in general, and the public at large.

Physicists and Biologists

For some time, ASTR had been lobbied to offer full membership to physicists and radiobiologists, many of whom held the view that without their participation in the organization, the American Society of Therapeutic Radiologists was incomplete. As soon as the project for writing a tentative

William T. Moss, president of ASTR in 1973–1974.

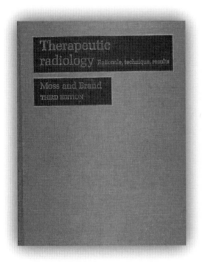

constitution and bylaws became known, Herman Suit, a member of the ad hoc committee, wrote to the president requesting again that physicists and radiobiologists be given full membership rather than associate memberships. At a meeting held on November 29, 1966, the membership discussed the matter, with Suit championing the cause for the physicists.

Warren Sinclair, the head of the Biophysics Department at M. D. Anderson Cancer Hospital, was at the meeting as a guest of James Nickson and was invited to present the argument for full membership. He pointed out that it would be an error for radiotherapists to disregard the contribution of physicists and radiobiologists to radiotherapy. In consequence, Sinclair said, physicists and radiobiologists should be offered full membership in the ASTR.[24]

The matter could not be put to a vote at that meeting because it would require a constitutional amendment.[25] However, an informal show-of-hands vote by the Board of Directors indicated that a majority of members disapproved of the measure.

Almost twelve years passed until Luther W. Brady, chairman of the Committee on Constitution and Bylaws, presented a document on membership for approval at a Board of Directors meeting held on April 28, 1978. It stated simply that "active full membership is presently reserved for physicians in the Americas who confine their professional practice to therapeutic radiology. In addition, it may be offered to radiation physicists, radiobiologists, and other allied health professionals who are fully involved in clinical practice of therapeutic radiology associated with and/or employed by a physician eligible for Active Membership."[26]

The proposal was unanimously passed by the Board of Directors on October 31, 1978, and approved by the membership the following spring. Radiation therapy physicists and radiation biologists would now be counted as active members.

The American Society of Therapeutic Radiologists' admittance of physicists to associate membership in the 1960s and full membership twelve years later was a positive measure of the organization's inclusiveness.

Government Grants

Another milestone in the evolution of radiotherapy as a medical specialty practice involved the development of programs aimed at providing training for a new generation of radiation therapists.

In the early 1960s, the National Cancer Institute actively supported training programs for radiation oncologists, radiobiologists, and radiation physicists, which many in the specialty pointed to as one of the accomplishments of the Committee for Radiation Therapy Studies (CRTS).[27] It also supported the development of nationally recognized research centers in radiation oncology, with twenty-six such centers ultimately being designated during the 1960s and 1970s as centers of excellence in radiation oncology.[28]

During the ensuing years, ASTR recognized that it was necessary to have highly trained therapeutic technologists if the field of therapeutic radiology was to develop to its fullest. In addition, the CRTS provided not only the means for setting national standards of practice in the field, but provided manuals, guidelines, and goals for the practice.[29]

For ASTR and the radiotherapy community, the 1960s were a time of solid achievement and growth. The society served as a platform for growth of the specialty, as well as an eloquent voice for the need for program development, a multiprotocol approach to oncology research and increased residency and training programs. The groundwork laid in the 1960s would pay dividend during the 1970s when the field of radiation therapy began to achieve critical mass.

Endnotes

1. *Record of Proceedings, American Society of Therapeutic Radiologists, Executive Committee Meeting*, April 14, 1966, p. 63.

2. Ibid.

3. Ibid, p. 66.

4. *Record of Proceedings, American Society of Therapeutic Radiologists*, November 28, 1965, p. 57.

5. *Record of Proceedings, American Society of Therapeutic Radiologists*, April 15, 1966, p. 65.

6. Luther W. Brady, MD, Simon Kramer, MD, Seymour H. Levitt, MD, Robert G. Parker, MD, and William E. Powers, "Radiation Oncology: Contributions of the United States in the Last Years of the 20th Century," *Radiology,* 2001; 219: 1–5, p. 6.

7. Ibid.

8. Ibid.

9. Ibid.

10. Ibid., p. 7.

11. David Hussey Tape-recorded Telephone Oral History Interview with Philip Rubin, Rochester, New York, October 7, 2003, p. 16.

12. Ibid.

13. Nancy Mendenhall Tape-recorded Oral History Interview with Theodore Phillips, n.d., p. 27.

14. Luther W. Brady, MD, Simon Kramer, MD, Seymour H. Levitt, MD, Robert G. Parker, MD, and William E. Powers, "Radiation Oncology: Contributions of the United States in the Last Years of the 20th Century," *Radiology,* 2001; 219: 1–5, p. 7.

15. Ibid, p. 8.

16. *Record of Proceedings, American Society of Therapeutic Radiologists, Annual Meeting*, December 7, 1960, p. 23.

17. *Record of Proceedings, American Society of Therapeutic Radiologists, Annual Meeting*, December 2, 1965, p. 60.

18. *Record of Proceedings, American Society of Therapeutic Radiologists, Luncheon Meeting*, April 11, 1968, p. 90.

19. *Record of Proceedings, American Society of Therapeutic Radiologists, Annual Meeting*, November 18, 1963, p. 46.

20. *Record of Proceedings, American Society of Therapeutic Radiologists, Bylaws*, July 1, 1968, p. 94.

21. David Hussey, Moshe Maor, and Luis Declos Tape-recorded Oral History Interview with Eleanor Montague, Houston, Texas, March 11, 2003.

22. *Record of Proceedings, American Society of Therapeutic Radiologists*, December 7, 1960, p. 23.

23. *Record of Proceedings, American Society of Therapeutic Radiologists*, April 8, 1959, p. 11.

24. *Record of Proceedings, American Society of Therapeutic Radiologists, Annual Dinner Meeting*, November 29, 1966, p. 72.

25. Ibid.

26. *Minutes, American Society of Therapeutic Radiologists, Board of Directors Meeting*, New Orleans, April 28, 1978, p. 1.

27. Luther W. Brady, MD, Simon Kramer, MD, Seymour H. Levitt, MD, Robert G. Parker, MD, and William E. Powers, "Radiation Oncology: Contributions of the United States in the Last Years of the 20th Century," *Radiology,* 2001; 219: 1–5, p. 7.

28. Ibid.

29. Raymond A. Gagliardi and J. Frank Wilson, *A History of the Radiological Sciences: Radiation Oncology* (Reston, Virginia: Radiology Centennial, Inc., 1996), p. 181.

Luther Brady, president of ASTR in 1972–73, was in charge of local arrangements at the society's first independent meeting at the Mountain Shadows Lodge in Scottsdale in 1970.

CHAPTER SIX

The Largest Society of Therapeutic Radiologists in the World

1970–1979

*I*f the 1960s had been an era of what at times seemed to be painfully slow growth for ASTRO, the 1970s were a period of rapid expansion of the society's membership as well as of its influence in the medical community. When the 1970s began, the organization was still known as the American Society for Therapeutic Radiologists (ASTR) and claimed slightly more than 300 members. When the decade ended in 1979, the ASTR had nearly quintupled its membership to 1,400 members, was sponsoring an official journal and was an increasingly respected voice in the growing oncology community.

Although the growth of the club was slow throughout the 1960s, it basically matched the growth of the specialty during this period. Relatively few physicians went into radiation therapy during the 1960s. Still, optimists saw a bright future. Although the increase of 56 new members from 252 in 1962 to 308 in 1970 could be considered glacial, charter members pointed out that the society was growing and was providing much-needed services to a specialty that was coming into its own. The number of institutions training residents in radiation therapy tripled between 1960 and 1970, reaching 66, and the number of residents in training increased more than sixfold, from 25 to 150.[1] The two educational pipelines for radiation therapy, i.e., straight radiation therapy residencies and general radiology residencies, would serve to provide new members to ASTR in the coming years.

In 1972, 500 residency positions in radiation therapy were offered in the United States, but only 244 were filled. Nevertheless, there was a clear need for more physicians in the field, a need fueled by the growing number of cancer patients and the number being referred for radiation therapy, as well as the increase in the number of radiation therapy departments across the country.[2]

As Americans lived longer, cancer was recognized to be more of a health threat than it had been considered in the past. By 1970, the

American people were demanding a cure for what was then the second leading cause of death in the United States. President Richard M. Nixon responded during his January 1971 State of the Union address by asking for an extra appropriation of more than $100 million "to launch an intensive campaign to find a cure for cancer." President Nixon declared that "the time has come in America when the same kind of concentrated effort that split the atom and took man to the moon should be turned toward conquering this dreaded disease."[3] In October 1971, the Army's Fort Dietrick, Maryland, biological warfare facility was converted to a cancer research center, eventually becoming the Frederick Cancer Research and Development Center. And on December 23, 1971, President Nixon followed through on his January promise to wage war on cancer when he signed the National Cancer Act into law.

With the nation mobilized for the new fight against cancer, the use of radiation as a treatment for the disease gained wider publicity. This would eventually be a contributing factor in the decision of many academic institutions to establish training programs in radiation therapy, thus contributing to the rapid membership growth of ASTR. Partly because of the impetus to offer radiation therapy training, the membership of ASTR doubled to more than 600 members between 1970 and 1973. Growth continued at a strong pace throughout the decade; by 1979 the number of members had grown to more than 1,400, including 100 associate members.

The rapid increase in membership numbers during the early 1970s was at least partly due to the conversion of the club (ACTR) to a society (ASTR), and ASTR's decision to host annual meetings and scientific sessions.

Mountain Shadows and the Biltmore, 1970–1972

The society's influence was heightened in 1970 when it began sponsoring its own scientific sessions on radiation therapy. For the first twelve years of the club and ASTR's existence, radiation therapy members of the Radiological Society of North America (RSNA) were asked each year to put together a radiotherapy program in conjunction with the RSNA annual meeting. In 1969, however, ASTR decided to hold its first independent scientific meeting. As a result, the first independent meeting of ASTR was held on November 11, 1970, at the Mountain Shadows Lodge in Scottsdale, Arizona, a suburb of Phoenix. The initial registration for this first separate national meeting was 308.

That meeting was an unqualified success. The focus of the meeting was a scientific program put on by established members of the society, faculty, and residents, who were given an opportunity to present research findings on a host of topics, including prostate cancer, cancer of the cervix, brachytherapy, and soft tissue cancers. There also were papers from members of the biology and physics community. The technical and scientific exhibits were almost nonexistent, but attendees enjoyed the social aspects of the meeting, which included a lengthy outdoor luncheon on the lawn of the Mountain Shadows Resort. Luther Brady recalled that he "was

An early ASTR panel discussion featured Luther Brady, Simon Kramer, and Gilbert Fletcher.

asked to be the chairman of the arrangements committee. Breakfast, lunch, and lodging were $36 per night."[4] There were too few rooms, and a number of members doubled up for the conference.

The Mountain Shadows scientific session was so successful that ASTR returned to the Phoenix area for similar sessions the next two years. In 1971 and 1972, the sessions were held at the Arizona Biltmore.

Luther Brady, who would later be sworn in as ASTR's president at the 1972 meeting, noted that the sessions took on a measure of formality during the three years they were held in the Phoenix area. "The second meeting was at the Arizona Biltmore Hotel in 1971. Bill Powers was the president that year. And that probably was the year in which things took on a more precise definition of what our goals and objectives were. The 1971 meeting was very much like an American Radium Society meeting. The scientific presentations were held in the morning, and the afternoon was free for informal kinds of discussions," Brady said.[5]

Topics for the scientific session of the society's annual meeting that year included a detailed symposium on prostate carcinoma, followed by a panel discussion on cervical lymph node metastases.[6] Thanks to Charles Honaker, then public relations director for the American College of Radiology, the symposium on prostate cancer was given wide coverage in *Hospital Practice,* a trade magazine serving the healthcare industry.[7]

Frank Wilson recalled going to the scientific meetings at the Biltmore and being impressed by the quality of the presentations. "All of the sessions were plenary," he said, "with lots of discussion after every presentation. It was a better format than the format we have today, with very competitive personalities who would play to the audience."[8]

Brady added that by the third meeting in Arizona, at the Biltmore in 1972, "things were evolving to where there was a fixed part of the program . . . and there also was a growing recognition that we were becoming more astute and more mature as an organization."[9]

The group also was making more demands on its host hotel. Brady remembered one incident at the Biltmore in 1972 in particular. "I was at that meeting, and I can still visualize today the afternoon of the cocktail party, which was on the green among the wings of the Arizona Biltmore Hotel, and the dinner was in the ballroom. Suddenly, it occurred to me that we had not made any arrangements to have wine at the dinner. But, the hotel staff was incredible. They took care of it in no time at all."[10]

Attendees at the 1972 Biltmore meeting also witnessed one of the most poignant presentations in ASTRO's history. Maurice Lenz, a Russian immigrant to the United States and longtime professor of radiology of the Columbia University College of Surgeons, was scheduled to address the dinner banquet at the Biltmore and give his recollections of his years at the *Fondation Curie* during the 1930s.[11] Lenz, however, had suffered a devastating stroke just six months before.

Brady had serious reservations about his esteemed colleague's ability to make his presentation to the society's annual banquet. But Anna Lenz assured Brady that her husband was well prepared for his speech. "He spoke at the dinner," Brady explained, "and he talked about the historical perspectives of the specialty, beginning primarily with the emphasis on the *Fondation Curie Institute* in Paris. And it was wonderful. He was terrific. He was charming, delightful, and humorous, with facts and photographs. He received a prolonged standing ovation. I thought that it was just a unique moment to have been able to allow him to have this moment in history for all the people who were there. He died not too long after that."[12]

That 1972 Biltmore meeting was a great success. It has often been cited as one of the seminal moments in ASTR's development.[13]

Maurice Lenz, professor of radiology at Columbia, gave a special address at the ASTR dinner banquet at the Arizona Biltmore Hotel in 1971.

The Red Journal

For ASTR to more fully represent the interests of radiation therapy, it needed to have an academic journal that would publish research by members and serve as a peer review vehicle for radiation therapists.

Shortly after the club formally became a society, the executive officers put the matter of an official journal to vote by the membership. The ASTR Board had appointed a committee to collect, review, and evaluate all options, and then the committee recommended an official journal to the Board. In August 1971, members voted overwhelmingly—339 to 17—to designate the journal *Cancer* as ASTR's official organ.[14] Long the official journal of the American Cancer Society, *Cancer* was one of the most respected medical journals in the nation in 1971, with a circulation of more than fifteen thousand. The ASTR Board did not require members to subscribe as a prerequisite for membership but noted that *Cancer* also served as the official organ for the James Ewing Society and the American Society of Clinical Oncologists.[15]

After four years, it became apparent to ASTR that, while *Cancer* was a perfectly suitable vehicle for disseminating news and research about radiation oncology, its universal global approach was perhaps too universal and too global for ASTR. For some time, there had been discussions about the need for a journal dedicated to radiation oncology issues. Philip Rubin was the driving force behind this effort. Throughout his career, Rubin worked to establish radiation oncology as a significant and important treatment area in oncology, and the journal was simply an outgrowth of his efforts to further the profession.

The *International Journal of Radiation Oncology*Biology*Physics (IJROBP)*, also known as the "Red Journal" because of its distinctive red cover, became the official publication of ASTRO. This publication made its first appearance in 1974. Herman Suit recalled "there was a substantial

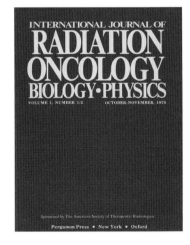

First issue of the Red Journal, November 1975.

A Half-Century of Past Presidents

ASTRO has been blessed with strong leadership over the years. Its presidents have come from every segment of the specialty. Most have devoted untold hours to the betterment of the society, giving up a year or two of their lives and careers in the process.

Juan del Regato, Gilbert Fletcher, and Henry S. Kaplan, the three cofounders, each served as president of the society, although none in the very early years. The society's first president, Simeon Cantril, was the only ASTRO president to die in office. All of those who served as president before 1971 are now deceased. The presidents and their terms are as follows:

1989

1958–1959	Simeon T. Cantril, MD	1983–1984	Gerald E. Hanks, MD
1959–1960	James W. J. Carpender, MD	1984–1985	Theodore L. Phillips, MD
1960–1961	Milton Friedman, MD	1985–1986	James D. Cox, MD
1961–1962	Manuel Garcia, MD	1986–1987	Robert W. Edland, MD
1962–1963	Isadore Lampe, MD	1987–1988	Lawrence W. Davis, MD
1963–1964	Franz J. Buschke, MD	1988–1989	Stanley E. Order, MD
1964–1965	Milford D. Schulz, MD	1989–1990	Carl R. Bogardus, MD
1965–1966	James J. Nickson, MD	1990–1991	Rodney R. Million, MD
1966–1967	Henry S. Kaplan, MD	1991–1992	Sarah S. Donaldson, MD
1967–1968	Gilbert H. Fletcher, MD	1992–1993	J. Frank Wilson, MD
1968–1969	Morton M. Kligerman, MD	1993–1994	Lester J. Peters, MD
1969–1970	Simon Kramer, MD	1994–1995	Jay R. Harris, MD
1970–1971	William E. Powers, MD	1995–1996	Steven A. Leibel, MD
1971–1972	Luther W. Brady, MD	1996–1997	Richard T. Hoppe, MD
1972–1973	Malcolm A. Bagshaw, MD	1997–1998	Larry E. Kun, MD
1973–1974	William T. Moss, MD	1998–1999	Christopher M. Rose, MD
1974–1975	Juan A. del Regato, MD	1999–2000	David H. Hussey, MD
1975–1976	Robert G. Parker, MD	2000–2001	David A. Larson, MD, PhD
1976–1977	Frank R. Hendrickson, MD	2001–2002	Nora A. Janjan, MD
1977–1978	Philip Rubin, MD	2002–2003	Joel E. Tepper, MD
1978–1979	Seymour H. Levitt, MD	2003–2004	Theodore S. Lawrence, MD, PhD
1979–1980	John W. Travis, MD	2004–2005	Prabhakar Tripuraneni, MD
1980–1981	Herman D. Suit, MD	2005–2006	K. Kian Ang, MD, PhD
1981–1982	Carlos A. Perez, MD	2006–2007	Louis B. Harrison, MD
1982–1983	Samuel Hellman, MD	2007–2008	Patricia J. Eifel, MD

Top: Three presidents of ASTRO during the 1980s: Carlos Perez, 1981–1982; Samuel Hellman, 1982–1983; and Gerald E. Hanks, 1983–1984.

Below: Four ASTRO presidents from the 1980s: Larry Davis, 1987–1988; Rodney Million, 1990–1991; Stanley Order, 1988–1989; and Carl R. Bogardus, 1989–1990.

Right: Four ASTRO presidents in the 1990s: Richard Hoppe, 1996–1997; Larry Kun, 1997–1998; Steve Leibel, 1995–1996; and Jay Harris, 1994–1995.

opinion that ASTRO should have its own journal, i.e., independent of the journal *Cancer*. I recall this very well, as I was one of several people strongly backing the *IJROBP* for ASTRO. Our need was for one high quality and strong journal. The discipline could not, at least then, support two journals."[16]

In addition to the Red Journal, there was discussion of producing a textbook on radiation oncology. The allocation of duties as to who would take responsibility for the Red Journal and who would shepherd the textbook through publication was determined by flipping an Eisenhower silver dollar. The person who picked "heads" got to do the journal and the person who picked "tails" got to do the book.[17] Rubin picked heads, and he became editor of the most successful journal on radiation therapy. Luther Brady, who drew tails, went on with Carlos Perez to edit one of the definitive textbooks in the specialty, *Principles and Practice of Radiation Oncology*.

The publication of the Red Journal began in 1974, and the following year, a contract was signed with Pergamon Press for its publication. During the mid-1970s, ASTR continued to support both the *IJROBP* and *Cancer*, but when ASTRO and Pergamon Press signed an exclusive agreement in 1984, the Red Journal became the society's official academic publication.[18]

When the *International Journal of Radiation Oncology*Biology*Physics* finally began publication, the editors and ASTR's Board engaged in much discussion as to content or focus of the new journal and to whom it should be directed. Rubin felt very strongly that the Red Journal should be an international publication. He realized that "one of the things that really bound us together was the collegiality which was quite strong. So I indicated that it shouldn't become an American journal. It was just not the way to do it."[19]

Another subject that Rubin felt strongly about was that biology and physics should also be prominent themes in the Red Journal. He noted that "science had to be a part of it. So I very deliberately constructed that and made a lot of contact with the biology group and always kept them involved. The key as to why it became successful was the fact that I succeeded in keeping those elements together."[20] Rubin remained as editor-in-chief of the Red Journal from 1974 until 1992, when he was succeeded by Jim Cox.

Rubin and Cox were determined to make the *IJROBP* the premier journal in the field of radiation oncology. Rubin recalled that "we didn't have to reject a lot of material because from the beginning, many of the articles were of a very, very high quality."[21]

The Red Journal published six issues during the first year, and twelve issues were published in the second year. Rubin and Cox were also successful in collecting advertisers to support and sponsor the Red Journal. But they were most proud of the fact that the quality of the articles was very high. They also noted that a significant number of the papers come from abroad. Rubin remarked that "there are many issues of the Red

*Philip Rubin, president of ASTR in 1977–78, was the editor of the International Journal of Radiation Oncology*Biology*Physics from its inception in 1974 until he stepped down in 1992.*

Carlos A. Perez, president of ASTRO in 1980–81, and Luther Brady edited the textbook Principles and Practice of Radiation Oncology.

Journal, where more than half the papers are international. I feel very keen about what we accomplished."[22] The *International Journal of Radiation Oncology*Biology*Physics* is one of the highest-rated journals in the cancer field and is consistently given high ratings by its peers.[23] In 1984, the Red Journal increased its publication schedule to fifteen issues per year.[24]

The *IJROBP* has also generated funds for the society that are used to support its research and educational activities. Rubin viewed the Red Journal's ability to generate interest in ASTR and its programs as a significant accomplishment.[25]

American College of Radiology (ACR)

From the beginning, intersociety relationships were important for ASTR. The American Club of Therapeutic Radiologists was born out of meetings at the Radiological Society of North America (RSNA) and American Radium Society (ARS). The strong relationships with these organizations have persisted over the years, as have the relationships with the American Association of Physicists in Medicine (AAPM) and the Society of Nuclear Medicine (SNM).

From the very start, however, the most critical relationship involved ASTR's relationship with the American College of Radiology (ACR). Management of ASTR's day-to-day affairs rested in the capable hands of staff from ACR after 1972. During this period, the ACR was responsible for management of the ASTR and staffing. Similarly the ASTR's headquarters was housed in the ACR office building. In addition, the ACR handled socioeconomic affairs of ACTR for many years.

Originally organized in 1923 as a purely honorary society, the ACR existed in a like fashion for more than a decade. Eventually, the leadership realized that socioeconomic concerns, even in those early days, required a broader and more politically active organization.[26] W. Edward Chamberlain, chairman of radiology at Temple University, became chairman of the new Board of Chancellors in 1935. He was given a clear mandate to reorganize the ACR as he saw fit. Ties were established to the other fledgling radiological societies, the ARS, RSNA, the American Roentgen Ray Society (ARRS), and the AMA. Liaisons were established between these societies and the new ACR allowing for formal dialogue between and among the different societies representing organized radiology.[27]

As other societies gained in membership over the years, they were allocated representation on the Board of Chancellors of the ACR. Radiation oncology was represented on the ACR Board by two chancellors, one nominated by ASTR and the other from the ARS. The Board representation gave a strong intersociety voice to radiation oncology.

For much of the 1970s and 1980s, ASTR's interface with the ACR came through the work of two remarkable women, Sheila Aubin in the Chicago office and later Frances Glica in the Philadelphia office. Aubin and Glica, both ACR administrative assistants, were "jills-of-all-trades," helping arrange ASTR conferences, writing the society's newsletter, posting checks and answering phones. ASTR officers quickly learned to rely on Aubin and Glica to get things done, no matter how outlandish the request.

"Sheila Aubin literally managed ASTR for ACR," recalled Seymour Levitt. "Phil Rubin was the first president to have a piano in his suite at the annual meeting. I said to Sheila that, 'when I'm president next year, I want a piano in my suite.' The next year, the meeting was at the Marriott in New Orleans. When I checked in, there was a little chocolate piano in my suite."[28] Even after ACR formalized its relationship with ASTRO in 1987, Aubin remained on as ASTRO's education staffer and meeting planner.

Fran Glica was a Philadelphia native who went to work as a secretary for ACR's John Curry in 1977. Herman Suit particularly remembered the work that John Curry did to make ASTRO run smoothly. "For my year as president, 1980–1981, and the meeting in Florida," Suit recalled, "John could not have been more effective and helpful. The society funds were quite limited and a reception was not feasible."[31] Curry somehow found money for the reception, accompanied Suit to a Miami liquor store, and helped the ASTRO president bring the refreshments up to his suite.

Carlos Perez passes the gavel to Herman Suit at the 1981 meeting in Miami.

The close relationship did not hide the fact that some members of ASTRO were somewhat dissatisfied with the affiliation. In a report published by Simon Kramer's Subcommittee on ASTRO/ACR Relations on September 28, 1985, some discontent was evident from questionnaires filled out by 1,047 members. That represented 46 percent of the total forms mailed. The survey documented very clearly that, among radiation oncologists, there was a decided lack of knowledge of the organizational structure, resources, programs, and activities of the ACR.[32]

Another area of concern noted in the survey was the lack of a separate identity given to radiation oncologists as compared to diagnostic radiologists within the ACR. This was particularly important to radiation oncologists as they reflected on their frequent lack of recognition as oncologists vis-à-vis medical oncologists.[33] Failure to make this distinction was a major source of dissatisfaction. Physicists within ASTRO and the ACR also expressed concern about a lack of support.

The report concluded with a series of recommendations designed to address the above-mentioned issues and strengthen the existing relationship between ASTRO and the American College of Radiology. In December 1987, the ASTRO Board approved a Management Services Agreement with the ACR to obtain administrative and support services. These measures indicated that both organizations recognized the mutual benefits that could be realized from the teamwork involved in the promotion of radiation oncology and radiation therapy.

With its record of membership growth and expansion of services, the 1970s were a decade of accomplishment for ASTR. An even bigger accomplishment during the decade was the society's role in establishing a strong identity for radiation oncology in the 1970s.

Endnotes

1. Raymond A. Gagliardi and J. Frank Wilson, *A History of the Radiological Sciences: Radiation Oncology* (Reston, Virginia: Radiology Centennial, Inc., 1996), p. 181.

2. Ibid.

3. Milestone (1971) *National Cancer Act of 1971*, dtp.nci.nih.gov/timeline/noflash/milestones/M4_Nixon.htm, p. 1.

4. Bill Beck Interview with Luther Brady and Seymour Levitt, p. 1.

5. Interview with Luther Brady, p. 30.

6. "Scientific Program for American Society of Therapeutic Radiologists," Arizona Biltmore Hotel, October 29, 30, and 31, 1971, pp. 1–4.

7. *ASTR Newsletter*, Spring 1972, p. 1.

8. Bill Beck Interview with J. Frank Wilson, p. 4.

9. Interview with Luther Brady, p. 30.

10. Ibid., p. 31.

11. Juan A. del Regato, *Radiological Oncologists: The Unfolding of a Medical Specialty*, pp. 249–250.

12. Interview with Luther Brady, p. 32.

13. Ibid., p. 33.

14. *ASTR Newsletter*, Fall 1971, p. 1.

15. *ASTR Newsletter*, Spring 1972, p. 1.

16. Herman Suit to Author, November 24, 2007.

17. Philip Rubin, Editorial, *International Journal of Radiation Oncology*Biology*Physics*, vol. 39, no. 4, 1997, p. 788.

18. Red Journal Contract, Appendix 1, Re: *International Journal of Radiation Oncology*Biology*Physics*, "Ownership," p. 1.

19. David Hussey Tape-recorded Telephone Oral History Interview with Philip Rubin, Rochester, New York, October 7, 2003, p. 11.

20. Ibid.

21. Ibid, p. 10.

22. Ibid., p. 12.

23. Ibid., p. 788.

24. Ibid.

25. Ibid., p. 11.

26. Raymond A. Gagliardi and J. Frank Wilson, *A History of the Radiological Sciences: Radiation Oncology* (Reston, Virginia: Radiology Centennial, Inc., 1996), p. 221.

27. Ibid.

28. Bill Beck Interview with Luther Brady and Seymour Levitt, p. 3.

29. Tape-recorded Oral History Interview with Frances Glica, Philadelphia, Pennsylvania, November 6, 2006, p. 2.

30. Ibid., p. 5.

31. Herman Suit to Author, November 24, 2007.

32. James D. Cox, MD, Robert W. Edland, MD, and H. K. Kerman, MD, "Report of the Subcommittee of the Board of Directors on ASTRO/ACR Relations," September 28, 1985, p. 1.

33. Ibid.

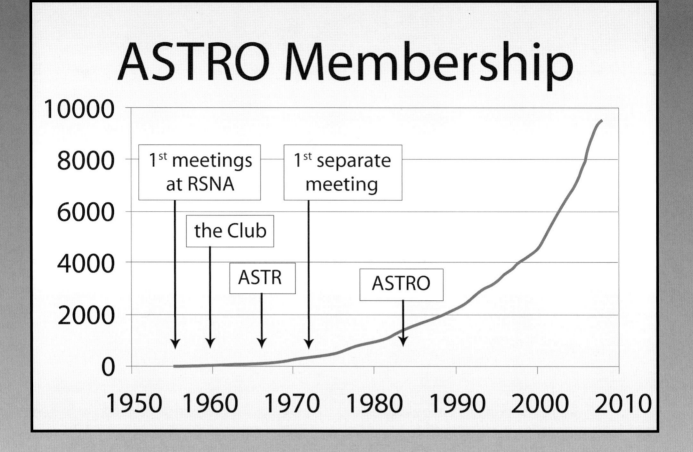

CHAPTER SEVEN

ASTR and the Emergence of Radiation Therapy in the 1970s

The 1970s were a defining moment for radiation therapy in the United States. The decade was characterized by major expansion in the practice of radiation therapy. A number of factors came together during the 1970s to encourage the growth of the field, including 1) the development of treatment policies based on a firm scientific foundation, 2) the separation of therapeutic and diagnostic radiology, 3) The dissemination of radiotherapy capabilities to cities throughout the country, 4) the emergence of a separate scientific society and journal for radiation oncology, and 5) demonstration of the efficacy of radiation therapy as a curative treatment modality for cancer patients. Radiation therapy blossomed in the United States during the 1970s largely because of these developments.

Radiotherapy's growing status was accompanied by a societal realization of the usefulness of radiation therapy as a tool in the growing battle against cancer. President Richard M. Nixon first raised the battle flags of the nation's commitment to fight cancer in 1972. However, the vast proportion of the $200 million to $500 million appropriated for the War on Cancer each year in the early to mid-1970s went to fund chemotherapy trials.[1] Very little money was used for research into improving the effectiveness of radiation therapy.

Development of Treatment Policies Based on a Firm Scientific Foundation

The late 1960s and the 1970s were characterized by the establishment of treatment policies based on fundamental physics and biological principles, a knowledge of the natural history of various cancers and their routes of spread, and a better understanding of the capabilities of the various treatment modalities available (surgery, chemotherapy, and radiation). Some of this work was done at M. D. Anderson Hospital where Gilbert Fletcher and the faculty in his department established firm treatment policies for treating a wide variety of cancers including head and neck, breast, gynecologic cancers, etc. This was derived from a periodic review of clinical results with emphasis on causes of failure, with modification of treatment policies as needed.

Similarly, at Stanford, Henry Kaplan and Malcolm Bagshaw led a talented group of faculty who took advantage of their access to the Western Hemisphere's first linear accelerator to report results for lymphoma, head and neck cancers, pediatric cancers, central nervous system tumors, and genitourinary cancers.

Karen K. Fu, a pioneer in head and neck cancer therapy.

Others made similar progress at many hospitals and medical schools around the United States and Canada during the 1970s. Names associated with advances in the early 1970s in specific areas include Henry Kaplan, Lillian Fuller, and Vera Peters in lymphomas; Gilbert Fletcher, Bob Lindberg, Rod Million, and C. C. Wang in head and neck cancers; Simon Kramer and Glenn Sheline in central nervous system tumors; Luis Delclos and Carlos Perez in gynecological cancers; Fletcher and Eleanor Montague in breast cancer; Giulio D'Angio in pediatric cancer; Len Gunderson in colorectal cancers, Herman Suit in sarcomas, Jack Maier in testicular cancer, Lowell Miller and Bill Caldwell in bladder cancer, and Malcolm Bagshaw, Juan del Regato, and Fred George in prostate cancer, and many others who are too numerous to name here. And many of those who made significant contributions to cancer management during the 1970s did not focus on just one or two specific cancers, but instead covered a broad range of areas.

The American Society of Therapeutic Radiologists (ASTR) encouraged the development of scientific research and showcased the results of this research at the society's annual scientific assembly each fall. By the time ASTR issued a call for the Seventeenth Scientific Assembly at the Hyatt Regency in San Francisco in October 1975, the amount and quality of scientific research and clinical trials submitted for presentation necessitated the scheduling of parallel sessions for the first time. Philip Rubin, ASTR's Program Committee chair, noted that "the scientific format is designed to allow for a wide range of formats including small informal group meetings, multiple small parallel sessions, and large plenary ses-

Luis Delclos, pioneer in gynecological cancers, and Eleanor Montague, pioneer in breast cancer.

sions."[2] Rubin noted that the 1978 session had attracted more than three hundred abstracts, and he asked all speakers to bring an audiotape and duplicate slides so that members attending wouldn't have to miss a presentation if there was a conflict with a parallel session.

Separation of Therapy and Diagnosis

A major development during the 1970s was the separation of radiology into two separate specialties, diagnostic radiology and therapeutic radiology. Prior to 1970, almost all persons practicing radia-

Vera Peters, pioneer in lymphomas and breast cancer.

Giulio D'Angio, a pioneer in pediatric radiation oncology.

tion therapy trained in general radiology. Some of them practiced both diagnostic radiology and therapy, some practiced only diagnostic radiology, and some practiced only radiotherapy. Some of these went on to receive further training in radiation therapy, either in the United States or Europe, but few trained exclusively in straight radiation oncology. There was a "sea change" almost overnight. After about 1973, almost no one going into therapy practice trained in general radiology and everyone trained in straight radiation therapy.

From 1949 to 1974, Juan del Regato trained fifty-five radiation therapy residents at Penrose Cancer Hospital. That alone doubled the number of practitioners who were in the field when del Regato began training residents in Colorado Springs following World War II.[3]

Bob Lindberg was one of those who was trained by del Regato in the 1960s. Lindberg inherited his interest in radiotherapy from his father, who practiced straight radiotherapy in Tucson from 1937 until his death in 1964. Soon after the American Board of Radiology (ABR) was set up in 1932, it began certifying in 1934 in therapeutic radiology alone as well as in diagnosis. Lindberg's father was one of the early radiologists certified in therapeutic radiology. Lindberg's father worked for Albert Soiland at the Los Angeles Tumor Clinic before opening his own practice in Tucson.[4]

Lindberg's introduction to radiotherapy wasn't a great deal more complicated than the training his father had experienced. "I was looking around for a residency with the idea of going back to Tucson to practice with my dad," Lindberg said. "I interned in Denver because it was close to Colorado Springs. I did a rotating internship at St. Luke's Hospital in Denver. Then I looked around and I got a straight therapy residency with del Regato in Colorado Springs at the Penrose Cancer Hospital. There were not many straight therapy residencies in 1959.[5] After going through three years with del Regato and one year of fellowship at Anderson, I realized that I was 'spoiled,'" Lindberg said. "I just couldn't see myself going back to Tucson into private practice."[6]

The separation of general radiology into two specialties (diagnostic and therapeutic radiology) is reflected in certification statistics from the American Board of Radiology. The ABR issued the first certificate for straight radiotherapy in 1934. However, most of those who practiced radiotherapy in the 1950s and 1960s were certified in general radiology. And the majority of the members of the American Club of Therapeutic Radiologists had general radiology certificates. Eleanor Quimby, a physicist member of ASTR, championed the need to examine radiologists and radiation therapists, requiring them to pass a section in physics to receive certification.

That all changed in the 1970s. After hovering at twenty to twenty-five certificates a year during the late 1960s, the number of straight radiotherapy certificates issued by the ABR went up dramatically during the early 1970s. The ABR issued only 19 certificates in straight therapeutic radiology in 1968. It issued 80 straight radiotherapy certificates in 1973, and that number climbed to almost 150 in 1974.[7]

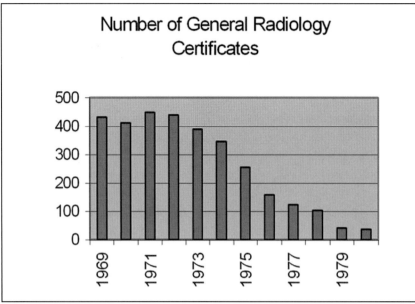

Number of General Radiology Certificates

By the end of the 1970s, most trainees pursuing a career in radiation therapy trained in straight radiation therapy, as evidenced by the decrease in general radiology certificates and the increase in straight radiation therapy certificates awarded by the American Board of Radiology.

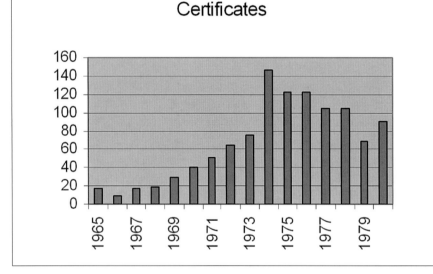

Number of Straight Radiotherapy Certificates

The ASTR had been lobbying for more representation in the certification process. Bill Powers was ASTR's president in 1970-1971 when the society formed a committee to convince the American Board of Radiology to add the ASTR as a sponsoring organization. Becoming a sponsoring organization would give the ASTR a voice in the selection of three trustees for the ABR. This would mean that radiation therapy would have six trustees instead of three. The other three were nominated by the American Radium Society (ARS). The addition of a sponsoring organization required unanimous approval of all of the current sponsors of the ABR. So the committee had to secure approval from five organizations: the AMA, Radiologial Society of North America (RSNA), American Roentgen Ray Society (ARRS), ARS, and the American College of Radiology (ACR).

Edith Quimby, pioneer physicist.

It also required unanimous approval of all of the current ABR trustees. When the vote was taken in 1973 for adding the ASTR as a sponsor, the ABR was meeting in New York City. "The only trustee missing was Bill Moss," Luther Brady explained. "He was in the process of moving from Chicago to Portland. I spent a couple of days trying to track Moss down. I had police looking for a black, four-door Buick with Illinois plates. They weren't able to find him, but we did get his vote eventually, and the ASTR did become a sponsor for the ABR. Lowell Miller, Juan del Regato, and I became ABR trustees, and the Board's composition doubled to six therapeutic radiologists."[8]

Brady recalled that "the next big issue was residency review. Residency Review Committees (RRCs) evaluate residency programs for accreditation; whereas Certification Boards evaluate individual physicians to assess their knowledge of the field. When I was appointed to the RRC in the 1970s, there was only one Residency Review Committee for all of radiology."[9]

This meant that diagnostic radiologists on the RRC would participate in decisions regarding the accreditation of radiation therapy programs and therapeutic radiologists on the RRC would participate in decisions regarding the accreditation of diagnostic radiology programs.

The change did not come then, but ultimately, the Residency Review Committee was split into two separate committees, one for diagnostic radiology and one for radiation oncology. The split occurred in the mid-1980s.[10] This not only improved the accreditation process for radiation oncology residencies, but it also made it easier to modify the radiation oncology program requirements to accommodate for changes in the specialty.

The growth of straight radiotherapy education, residencies, fellowships, and certification during the 1970s was an important factor for the separation of the field from the practice of diagnostic radiology. The gradual separation of diagnostic and therapeutic radiation into departments and sections at most medical schools and teaching hospitals was probably the most important development leading to the establishment of an identity for the specialty. As a result, radiation oncology was finally emerging from the shadow of the parent specialty.

Radiation Therapy Facilities

Another thing that began in the 1970s was the proliferation of radiation therapy facilities. Technology that was available only at certain specialized academic centers at the beginning of the decade became available in many communities around the country by the end of the decade. This was partly due to the availability of reasonably priced megavoltage equipment, e.g., cobalt-60, low-energy linear accelerators, simulators, and rudimentary treatment planning computers. However, it also was due to the introduction of Medicare in 1965 and subsequent improved reimbursement for radiation therapy services

With the improvement of therapeutic equipment and techniques during the immediate postwar period, radiotherapy enjoyed sustained growth.

Memorial Sloan-Kettering Hospital's Department of Radiation Therapy in New York City, for example, nearly doubled its patient load between the early 1950s and 1960s, a rate of increase that was matched by many other institutions in the United States. And the growth rate accelerated between the mid-1960s and the mid-1970s.

The growth in patient load led many in the field to wonder where the next generation of therapeutic radiologists would come from. The number of institutions offering training in radiation therapy increased to sixty-six from 1960 to 1970 and to 107 by 1978. The number of residency positions available also increased from 150 in 1970 to 244 by 1972.[11]

By 1978, there were 344 residents in training in straight radiotherapy, which was an all-time high. However, there also were some worrisome trends. For one thing, only about half the 595 available positions were filled.[12] Graduates of US medical schools were also increasing at unprecedented rates in the 1970s. But the new graduates weren't flocking to the specialty.

Medical schools also went through a dramatic growth spurt in the 1960s and 1970s. There were only 9 new medical schools opened between 1926 and 1960. Twenty-three new schools opened in the 1960s, and another 13 opened in the 1970s. After reaching a high of 107 institutions with radiotherapy programs in 1978, the number of medical schools offering training in straight radiotherapy dropped off to 89 in 1982.[13]

When Bob Lindberg did his fellowship at M. D. Anderson Hospital in 1963, he was impressed by the wide variety of equipment available at that institution. "In the basement," he said, "we had an old Allis-Chalmers 22 MeV betatron, and Nora Tapley was using electrons on an 18 MeV Siemens betatron. There was the Grimmett cobalt unit, a rotating AECL cobalt unit, and a cesium head and neck unit on the ground floor. And up on the second floor there were four to six 250 kV units."[14] There were a few academic centers that were well equipped in the 1960s, but most radiotherapy departments had limited capabilities.

That changed in the 1970s. By 1975, linear accelerators were becoming widely available throughout the United States, many with both megavoltage X-ray beams and electrons, and most institutions had simulators, treatment planning computers, and afterloading brachytherapy capabilities. Some institutions continued to have cobalt machines and betatrons in the late 1970s, but those machines were becoming less sustainable.

In the fall of 1975, ASTR surveyed its membership, and more than 300 members returned the survey. This gave the ASTR a glimpse of the state of the technology at the time. Members reported that they were using 672 megavoltage units, 535 other treatment machines, and 138 simulators.[15]

The proliferation of radiation therapy facilities and equipment meant a need for more radiotherapy technologists as well as therapeutic radiologists. This was a major concern in the 1970s. In November 1977, the society went on record as opposing proposed reimbursement regulations promulgated by the Health Resources Administration that would unnecessarily penalize institutions engaging in training and research, those training the next generation

Two presidents in the 1970s. Frank R. Hendrickson (1976–1977) and Philip Rubin in 1977–1978.

of radiotherapy technologists, "as there is a desperate need for more manpower at the technical and medical level."[16] Frank Hendrickson, who was chairman of the ASTR Board that year, pointed out that fewer patients could be treated on a given piece of machinery in a research institution than in a clinical care setting. "In general," he said, "it is most difficult to determine the number of treatment visits or number of treatments in a year in an easy, well defined way."[17] The new regulations, he said, would cut reimbursements for the institutions that needed them the most.

Furthermore, Hendrickson noted, "technological advances beyond the cobalt-60 and betatron machines of the past have led to increased use of radiation therapy for patients previously not treated for a cure."[18] At the time, Herman Suit was polling a number of cancer specialists regarding the impact high-energy radiation therapy equipment had on cure rates for a wide variety of cancers. The response to Suit's survey reinforced Hendrickson's point that the new radiotherapy equipment did lead to better results.

In the early 1980s, ASTR became involved in planning how to train the hundreds of new radiation therapy technologists who would be needed to operate and maintain the new generation of equipment. The society's Committee on Technology Affairs, chaired by Robert H. Sagerman, plowed new ground with its painstaking study of the problem and potential solutions.[19]

ASTR worked with a number of different federal agencies on making radiation therapy as safe as possible for patients and practitioners. In 1977, the society worked closely with the Nuclear Regulatory Commission in establishing regulations for the medical use of the byproduct material from

nuclear reactors, including radioactive isotopes and radiopharmaceuticals in radiotherapy practice.[20]

Advancements in technology were described in great detail in sessions and symposia during ASTR's annual scientific assembly in those years. In 1978, attendees heard Norah Tapley's discussion of "Clinical Applications of the 7-25 MeV Electron Beam," Robert Stewart's "Rationale and Status of Particle Radiation Therapy," and "Computerized Tomography in Radiation Treatment Planning" by James M. Slater and William T. Chu.[21]

In addition, ASTR worked closely with the Radiation Therapy Oncology Group (RTOG) to coordinate a number of research projects during the decade, including studies on radiation therapy sensitizers and protectors, high LET radiation, hyperthermia, and radioactively labeled immunoglobulins.[22] In 1982, ASTR worked closely with RTOG to sponsor an international workshop in Houston, Texas, on scientific progress in the physics and engineering of particle beams and the investigation of their biological properties.[23]

The introduction of new radionuclides in the wake of the first nuclear chain reactions in the mid-1940s revived the practice of brachytherapy, with the availability of hermetically sealed artificially produced radionuclides in tubes, needles, capsules, or other configurations and inserting them in the vicinity of tumors. Brachytherapy use had declined in the 1950s after the introduction of megavoltage external beam capabilities, but the growing sophistication of nuclear reactors in the late 1950s and 1960s renewed interest in brachytherapy for interstitial, intracavitary, and surface applications.[24]

Brachytherapy was long supported by the ASTR. In 1978, the society firmly restated its policy toward the sometime controversial treatment. "The use of brachytherapy is an integral part of the total program of radiation therapy," ASTR said, "and as such, when it is in the best interest of the patient, brachytherapy should be carried out by the radiation therapist(s) responsible for total radiation therapy management of the patient."[25]

The explosion in technological innovation and new techniques between 1957 and 1980 and beyond made it possible for ASTR and its members to establish more effective treatment regimens for cancer during the final two decades of the twentieth century.

A Society and Journal for Radiation Oncology

Another factor that contributed to the tremendous expansion of the field of radiation therapy in the 1970s was the development of instruments to convey scientific knowledge of the field. This was achieved by the formation of the ASTR and the establishment of the *International Journal of Radiation Oncology*Biology*Physics*.

The formation of the ASTR was a giant step forward. Radiation therapy now had its own separate organization for continuing medical education of therapeutic radiologists, radiotherapy technologists, and residents; to encourage and report research results; and to represent the specialty to the rest of medicine and the public.

ASTR matured as a full-fledged medical society during the 1970s, encouraging scientific research and clinical trials, introducing continuing education programs, enrolling members at a record pace, and supporting the separation of diagnosis and therapy.

In 1984, ASTRO's Board began discussions about creating a journal owned by the society and interviewed various publishers to ascertain interest. "I took the viewpoint the field really didn't need another journal," Cox said. "It would dilute the work of the Red Journal. ASTRO was in deep trouble financially and couldn't afford a new journal."[26]

When Robert Maxwell, the owner of Pergamon Press, agreed to pay ASTRO $69,000 yearly royalty for the privilege of publishing the Red Journal, the Board agreed that the Red Journal would become the official journal of the society. "The Red Journal had a structure, a track record and was going to give money to ASTRO," Cox said. "It was a fairly easy decision to make."[27]

The formation of the ASTR and the Red Journal were particularly important developments because one of the principal steps in establishing an identity for a specialty is the demonstration of a distinct research/educational society and a specific journal for the specialty.

The establishment of ASTR and the Red Journal was perhaps the most visible manifestation of the maturation of the field of radiation oncology during the 1970s. The growth of ASTR and its programs was a natural outgrowth of radiation therapy's growing prominence in the medical community's approach to treating cancer.

Endnotes

1. Clinton Leaf and Doris Burke, "Why We're Losing the War on Cancer," *Fortune,* March 22, 2004.

2. Philip Rubin, "To My Colleagues," July 1, 1978, p. 1.

3. Raymond A. Gagliardi and J. Frank Wilson, *A History of the Radiological Sciences: Radiation Oncology* (Reston, Virginia: Radiology Centennial, Inc., 1996), pp. 180–181.

4. Interview with Bob Lindberg, p. 40.

5. Ibid., p. 3.

6. Ibid., p. 4.

7. David Hussey, American Board of Radiology Straight Radiotherapy Certificates, 1965–1980, Slide 2.

8. Bill Beck Interview with Luther Brady and Seymour Leavitt, p. 3.

9. Ibid.

10. Interview with Luther Brady, p. 40.

11. Raymond A. Gagliardi and J. Frank Wilson, *A History of the Radiological Sciences: Radiation Oncology* (Reston, Virginia: Radiology Centennial, Inc., 1996), p. 181.

12. Ibid.

13. Ibid.

14. Interview with Bob Lindberg, p. 4.

15. *American Society for Therapeutic Radiologists Survey*, Fall 1975, p. 1.

16. Frank R. Hendrickson, chairman, American Society for Therapeutic Radiologists, letter to the Office of Planning, Evaluation and Legislation, Health Resources Administration, November 8, 1977, p. 2.

17. Ibid.

18. Ibid.

19. *Minutes of the American Society for Therapeutic Radiologists Committee on Technology Affairs*, August 1980, pp. 1–4.

20. Frederick W. George III, University of Southern California, letter to Leo Wade, Jr., MD, US NRC, June 6, 1977, pp. 1–3.

21. *American Society for Therapeutic Radiologists, Packet IV*, July 1, 1978, pp. 1–12.

22. *ASTR Newsletter*, "Items of Interest," Fall 1981.

23. *ASTR Newsletter*, vol. 1, no. 2, p. 8.

24. Raymond A. Gagliardi and J. Frank Wilson, *A History of the Radiological Sciences: Radiation Oncology* (Reston, Virginia: Radiology Centennial, Inc., 1996), pp. 194–195.

25. *ASTR Newsletter*, January 1978, p. 4.

26. Ibid., p. 3.

27. Ibid.

Simon Kramer, president of the ASTR in 1969–1970.

CHAPTER EIGHT

ASTR in a Decade of Change

1972–1982

The decade of the 1970s was an era of growth and expansion for the American Society of Therapeutic Radiologists. What had been an informal club during the period 1958 to 1966 had become a full-fledged society offering a growing number of members increasingly sophisticated annual conferences, continuing education courses, and two official journals, the *International Journal for Radiation Oncology*Biology*Physics* and *Cancer.* Under the leadership of society presidents, including Simon Kramer, Bill Powers, Luther Brady, Malcolm Bagshaw, Bill Moss, Juan del Regato, Bob Parker, Frank Hendrickson, Philip Rubin and Seymour Levitt, ASTR kept pace with the progress being made in the field of radiotherapy.

In 1971, the American Federation of Clinical Oncologic Societies (AFCOS) formally admitted ASTR to its membership. Other members of AFCOS included the American Radium Society, the American Association for Cancer Education, American Society of Clinical Oncology, the James Ewing Society, the Society of Gynecologic Oncologists, and the Head and Neck Surgical Society.[1] AFCOS described itself as a coalition of professional oncology societies concerned with quality healthcare delivery, access to care, and the education of patients, healthcare providers, legislators, and the general public.

By 1972, ASTR membership had grown to more than 740 members, and the society had significantly improved the quality of its annual scientific sessions at the annual meeting. The popularity of the scientific sessions gave even more impetus to the membership process. The ASTR Board received 137 applications for membership in January 1973.[2]

The society also began in 1973 to seriously consider changing its name. The most popular choice among the members was the American Society for Radiation Oncology. But the term *radiation oncology* wasn't as generally accepted in the early 1970s as it is today. It wasn't until 1983 that ASTR actually did change its name, and the name chosen wasn't ASRO.[3]

The growth of the field in the early 1970s also was illustrated by a move to establish de facto state chapters. Frank Ellis reported to the ASTR Board in early 1973 that a group in Wisconsin proposed to establish a statewide radiation therapy society.[4] Radiation therapists in other states, including New York, Pennsylvania, and California, formed ad hoc state societies during the mid-1970s.

As the decade wore on, membership in ASTR continued to grow. Following the 1974 annual conference at Key Biscayne, Florida, 122 membership applications were approved, bringing total membership to 966.[5]

One measure of the growth of the society was the complexity of its committee structure, which increased considerably during this period. By the mid-1970s, ASTR had fifteen standing committees, including Local Arrangements, Audio-visual Services, Constitution and Bylaws, Nominating, Program, Radiation Physics and Biology, Membership, and Editorial. Other committees were responsible for Education and Training, Medical Economics, Private Practice, Professional Liability, Professional Standards, Projections, Public Relations, and Technology Committees. ASTR also appointed an Advisory Committee for the distribution of the Anna Hamann Estate, money bequeathed to ASTR for the support of the education of women and foreign students in radiation therapy. There was also an ASTR Council to interact with the American College of Radiology, and there were liaisons to a number of other societies.[6]

Seymour H. Levitt, president of ASTR in 1978–1979.

Another measure of ASTR's maturity was the growth of its budget, which increased from $15,000 in 1970 to $140,000 in 1979. In 1974, there was a dues increase to $25 a year for full members and $10 a year for associate and corresponding members.[7] Although this seems minuscule today, $25 a year was a sizable amount at a time when the median household income was $11,800 a year and a gallon of gasoline cost fifty cents. William T. Moss, ASTR's president in 1973–1974, pointed out that the increase was necessary if the society was to keep even with inflation.

Radiation therapy also was gaining credibility in the eyes of the nation's medical/scientific establishment. In 1974, the National Cancer Institute awarded a $1.5 million grant to the American College of Radiology to evaluate existing methods of radiation treatment for cancer and to establish Patterns of Care guidelines for examination of the national practice with regards to the structure and processes of care that were employed, as well as related outcomes. The project was called the Patterns of Care Study (PCS). ASTR President Moss and Chairman Malcolm Bagshaw were kept fully informed of PCS results when former ASTR President Simon Kramer was named to direct the three-year project for ACR.

Malcolm A Bagshaw, president of the ASTR in 1972–1973.

The PCS was administered through ACR's Philadelphia office, and John Curry, who was in charge of the office at the time, became the first executive director of the program. Both the PCS feasibility grant and the first Radiation Therapy Oncology Group (RTOG) grant were initially handled within the Jefferson Grant Office. Both were moved to be within the structure of ACR, with the help of Bill Powers and Luther Brady. The

ACR created a Philadelphia Office to administer both RTOG and PCS. A Committee on PCS was created and seated within the Commission on Radiation Oncology, chaired at that time by Bill Moss.

"Patterns of Care looked at the quality of radiation oncology care in the United States," Curry said. "It was a very powerful tool. All those residents we hired as investigators subsequently developed into the ASTRO leadership. It's amazing how many of the ASTRO chairmen in the 1990s and twenty-first century were involved initially with the Philadelphia office and the PCS."[8]

The PCS conducted facility and outcome surveys. The former documented the location of radiation therapy programs, equipment available, and manpower issues. The later analyzed the evaluation, treatment, and follow-up of patients with selected cancers to develop an indicator of national standards. The diseases that were surveyed included Hodgkin's disease, laryngeal cancer, cervical cancer, and other carcinomas. These surveys were conducted by residents in radiation therapy programs around the country and included such future ASTRO notables as Steve Leibel, Ralph Weichselbaum, and Rich Hoppe.

ASTR was very helpful in allowing PCS to have several site-specific committee meetings during the society's annual meetings. Several radiation oncologists participated in the different working committees of PCS and were very helpful in the surveys and analysis of the results.

Patterns of Care continues to this day as the Quality Research in Radiation Oncology Project with J. Frank Wilson as principal investigator. Radiotherapy remains one of the first medical specialties in the nation to develop a mechanism to evaluate the quality of care delivered by its practitioners throughout the nation.[9]

Robert G. Parker, president of the ASTR in 1975–1976.

In 1976, ASTR's Public Relations and Audio-visual Committees unveiled a ten-minute, 16 mm film explaining radiotherapy to the general public. This project had been championed by Robert G. Parker, ASTR's president in 1975–1976. Produced under the auspices of ASTR and the American College of Radiology, the film titled *Radiation: The Cancer Fighter* was widely distributed to public media outlets in the spring of 1977. It was awarded a first prize in the annual film festival sponsored by the American Medical Writers Association.

For three years, at the annual meeting, the ASTR offered an opportunity for residents to have breakfast with leaders in the field. These were informal sessions on three consecutive days that included, for example, Gilbert Fletcher talking about head and neck cancer, Victor Marcial on cervical cancer, and Henry Kaplan on lymphomas. Word got out to the general membership, who stood in the doorways to hear what the masters had to say. Meanwhile, the residents sat comfortably around tables with pastries and coffee!

Given the popularity of these early morning sessions, ASTR broadened its continuing education programs in 1976, offering a postgraduate education program of refresher courses at the October 1976 ASTR meeting in Atlanta. Courses in radiobiology and physics were offered along with sessions on Non-Hodgkin's Lymphomas, Hematologic Malignancies, Neck Nodes, Combined Treatment, Pre-treatment Surgical Staging in Cancer of the Cervix, and Bone Tumors.[10]

ASTR also made its voice heard in the increasingly complex debate about delivery of healthcare. When the Carter administration's Health Resources Administration issued its *Guidelines for the Development of Criteria and Standards for Radiation Therapy Services by Health Systems Agencies* in 1977, ASTR's Board of Directors asked Chairman Frank Hendrickson to respond on behalf of the society. Hendrickson wrote to commend the Department of Health, Education, and Welfare for its efforts to support the development of national guidelines. But he cautioned the health planners about a "one size fits all approach" to treating cancer. Populations in their sixties have ten times the cancer incidence of populations in their thirties and forties, he said. Hendrickson urged federal support of the "use of radiation therapy for patients not previously treated with radiotherapy," including victims of Hodgkin's disease, prostate and breast cancer, colon cancer, and many pediatric cancers.[11] Hendrickson also pointed out "there is a desperate need for more manpower at the technical and medical level, and more basic information on ways to manage cancer patients."[12]

Frank R. Hendrickson, president of the ASTR in 1976–1977.

Following the society's 1978 meeting, James Cox reported to the ASTR Board that their membership had surpassed 1,000 for the first time. Cox, the head of the ASTR Membership Committee, noted that the ASTR had 1,082 active members, 86 associate members, 87 junior members, and 11 retired members.[13] The growth in membership, however, didn't mean that ASTR and the field of radiotherapy would take its seat at the table of elite organizations governing American medicine. In 1978, the American Medical Association turned down a request for House of Delegate representation for the ASTR, ruling that there weren't enough ASTR members in the AMA. In an effort to correct this problem, Luther Brady urged all of his colleagues in the ASTR to consider joining the AMA.[14]

Perhaps the most significant measure of how far ASTR had come in a decade's time was contained in the mid-year 1979 treasurer's report. Lawrence W. Davis noted that the society had almost $140,000 cash on hand.[15] That was nearly two-and-a-half times the $58,000 the society had on hand just two years earlier. Thanks to intelligent cost-cutting measures instituted by Presidents Philip Rubin and Seymour Levitt, ASTR would enter the 1980s on a firm financial footing.

The Growth of Experimental Technologies

The 1970s and early 1980s were years when the specialty did look at many new (and experimental) technologies, e.g., hyperbaric oxygen, carboxygen, fast neutrons, pi mesons, heavy charged particles, radiosensitizers, radioprotectors, hyperthermia, and protons. Many of these new technologies never panned out, for one reason or another, but some have become an accepted part of practice, and some are still being evaluated.

Eric Hall was awarded the ASTRO Gold Medal for his work in radiation biology research and teaching in 1993.

Zvi Fuks, ASTRO Gold Medal Award winner in 1996.

Gold Medal winners Eleanor Montague and Carlos Perez with their spouses at the Gold Medal dinner in 1992.

One of the strengths of the specialty has been its willingness to look at new technologies, to evaluate them scientifically, and then accept or reject them on their merits.

ASTR made gigantic strides during the 1970s, in the encouragement of scientific research, clinical medicine, and the development of technology. Those in the field showed a willingness to push the envelopes of scientific research and clinical medicine even further, in the constant quest to make radiotherapy an even more potent weapon in the war against cancer.

ASTR emerged from the 1970s as a growing medical society formed to give voice to those who practiced radiation therapy on the front lines of the nation's battle against cancer. Both the practice and the ASTR would continue to grow and evolve in the 1980s, as the equipment and techniques employed became ever more sophisticated and the specialty continued to grow in numbers and influence.

The Gold Medal

In 1976, then ASTR President Robert G. Parker suggested that the society should inaugurate a Gold Medal Award to recognize the men and women who had made great contributions to radiation therapy and to ASTR. Parker's suggestion, which was acted upon favorably by the ASTR Board, ignited intense lobbying among the supporters of Juan del Regato, Gilbert Fletcher, and Henry Kaplan. Parker suggested that the decision of selecting the first nominee should rest on the shoulders of Frank Hendrickson, the incoming 1976–1977 president of ASTR.

Hendrickson delegated Parker, his predecessor, with the responsibility of forming the rules for the award and selecting the first nominee.

"I decided that all three, del Regato, Fletcher, and Kaplan were equally deserving and so decided to award three medals," Parker said. "Then, the problem became the order of presentation because it might be considered the first person named was the first ever to receive the gold medal."[16]

Luther Brady, 1987 Gold Medal winner; Seymour Levitt; and European colleague Harry Bartelink at an ASTRO Gold Medal dinner.

Herman Suit awarding the ASTRO Gold Medal to Morton M. Kligerman in 1982.

Parker came up with what he thought was an elegant solution to the problem. He decided to call the three nominees in alphabetical order to inform them of their award.[17]

That first award of the ASTR Gold Medal in 1977 began a tradition of honoring those in the field whose contributions advanced the field of radiation therapy. Two of Parker's mentors, Franz J. Buschke (1978) and Isadore Lampe (1979) were Gold Medal recipients, and Parker himself was awarded a Gold Medal in 1989.

From 1978 to 1980, two winners of the Gold Medal were announced each year, and from 1981 to 1989, ASTRO only awarded one Gold Medal each year. Since 1990, ASTRO has awarded at least two and in some years three (1993, 2002, 2003, 2004) Gold Medals.

ASTRO's awarding of the Gold Medal was recognition of the importance of the pioneers in the society's past. ASTRO's focus on strategic planning in the 1980s was recognition of the importance of the society's future. And increasingly, that future would be involved with socioeconomic issues, especially following the society's move to suburban Washington, DC, in the 1990s.

Gold Medalists in 2004: Paul Wallner, Eli Glatstein, and Luka Milas.

ASTR Headquarters

The American College of Radiology executive offices were located in Chicago in the early 1970s, but the ACR also maintained a satellite office in Chevy Chase, Maryland. However, when the ACR received two large research grants from the National Cancer Institute in the mid-1970s to support PCS and to fund the establishment of the Radiation Therapy Oncology Group, and the ACR Board determined that the grants would be better administered if an independent office handled that function. Thus, the ACR opened the office in Philadelphia in 1977 to administer the National Cancer Institute (NCI) grants and the RTOG.

The Philadelphia office would become the ASTR headquarters from 1977 to 1998. John Curry, longtime executive director of the American College of Radiology and a 2002 ACR Gold Medal recipient, operated ACR's office in Philadelphia during the late 1970s. As such, he was responsible for the administration of ASTR under the terms of the agreement ASTR had signed with the ACR early in the decade. Curry had been Simon Kramer's administrator at Jefferson Hospital in Philadelphia and then executive director of the RTOG before joining the ACR in 1977. Curry would go on to become the ACR's executive director in 1984, a position he held until he retired in 2002. He was made an honorary member of ASTRO in 2002, the highest honor the society can bestow on a nonmember.

The 1972 Management Services Agreement with the ACR was signed by then ASTR President Luther Brady. It allowed ASTR to retain its independence, but for a fixed annual fee, ASTR received services it couldn't afford to provide in a self-management framework. From 1977 to 1998, ACR provided ASTR with member communications, coordination of the annual scientific meeting, and editing and publishing the *ASTRO Newsletter* after 1982.

For many longtime ASTR/ASTRO members, Frances Glica was the society's face and voice during the 1970s and 1980s. Frances Glica was born and raised in Philadelphia, and she served as ASTRO's executive secretary for more than twenty years. Curry hired Glica to be his secretary in their Philadelphia office in 1977, shortly after the office opened.

Glica remembered that "the Philadelphia office was in the Edison Building located on Ninth Street between Chestnut and Walnut, actually Ninth and Sansom. It was a very strange affair. The first day that I worked for the ACR, the desk that I had was falling apart."[18] The headquarters was eventually moved a block down the street to the Pennsylvania Manufacturers Association Building at Tenth and Chestnut.

Soon after being hired, Curry sent Glica to Bethesda, Maryland, where the ACR held meetings periodically. The ACR had received the large grant from the NCI, so she was asked to take the minutes of

John Curry and Sarah Donaldson, ASTRO president 1991–1992. John Curry, as executive director of the ACR, was responsible for the administration of ASTRO in its early years.

Frances and Richard Glica. Fran Glica served as ASTRO's executive secretary for more than twenty years.

the meetings that were held to administer that grant. In 1982, Glica was given the additional duties of associate editor of the *ASTRO Newsletter* when the society's Long-range Planning Committee decided to upgrade the old newsletter. Prior to 1982, the newsletter had been published in ASTRO's Chicago office, but since the organization was growing, the additional work was transferred to Philadelphia. While working in the Philadelphia office, Glica remembered that "we were also responsible for the Council of Regional Radiation Oncology Societies (CARROS), which eventually became a chapter of the ACR."[19]

Prior to Glica's arrival, Sheila Aubin, who was employed by the American College of Radiology in its Chicago office, handled all of ASTR's affairs under the terms of the Management Agreement between the ACR and the society. After Glica came on board, Aubin continued to assist ASTR with its meeting planning and member services, but Glica handled all of the other ASTR staff duties. In the mid-1980s, Glica took over the work for CARROS and assumed duties for the Long-range Planning Committee.

By then, John Curry had been named executive director of the ACR and had moved the ACR executive office to Reston, Virginia. Curry brought Nick Croce from Cooper Hospital, where he served as the Radiation Oncology Department administrator, to head the Philadelphia office of the ACR. Nick Croce would eventually become responsible for the management of ASTRO in 1987. Croce was executive director of ASTRO until 1995, when he was replaced by an interim director. In 1997, Frank Malouff assumed responsibility as executive director.

"Nick Croce wore two hats," explained Kathy Thomas, who came to work for the ACR in 1990 and transferred over to the staff of ASTRO in 1995. "He was a Philadelphia kid who had actually attended the seminary. Nick was amazingly bright, and charismatic. But he was also a streetwise Philly guy. He and John Curry were all Simon Kramer apprentices at Thomas Jefferson in Philadelphia."[20]

In 1986, Glica became executive secretary of ASTRO and began staffing the Board meetings and working on various other committees. Glica recalled she "was never involved in meeting planning. My sole responsibility was working as ASTRO's executive secretary, and by then, we had moved to the ARA Tower 4 at Eleventh and Market. In the early 1990s, it was decided to move the ASTRO office function to Reston, Virginia, although I remained in Philadelphia."[21]

During much of the 1970s and 1980s, the ASTR staff consisted of Curry and Glica, later Croce and Glica, part-time clerical help and administrative support from Sheila Aubin in Chicago, as needed. Gregg Robinson, who had worked as a dosimetrist under Luther Brady at Hahnemann Hospital in Philadelphia, was brought into the Philadelphia office of ASTRO after Curry and Croce left for their new jobs with ACR in Reston.[22]

By 1989, Glica was contemplating retirement. She began working part time starting in 1990 and did so for the next eight years. "I worked full time from 1977 to 1989, and then part time from 1990 to 1998," she recalled. "I'm now retired, but I still attend the annual meeting because they made me an honorary member. I was also the last ASTRO employee in Philadelphia."[23]

Glica's two decades with ASTRO left her with strong opinions about the direction that the society has taken and will take in the future. She noted that "the society has switched from a strictly scientific and educational focus to more of a socioeconomic focus. The idea had been that radiation oncology was a subset of radiology, and the ACR handled socioeconomic matters for radiology. However, there was always a feeling within ASTRO that the ACR wasn't prepared to give radiation oncology the service it needed. It was obvious that the split was going to happen, but it was kind of surprising when it actually did happen because they had talked about it for so long, and nobody had ever done anything about it."[24]

Glica's tenure in the Philadelphia office spanned the period in which ASTR changed its name to ASTRO. This occurred in 1982 during the presidency of Carlos Perez. The name change was significant in that it recognized the transition from a derivative of radiology to the independent specialty of radiation oncology. The renamed society would for the first time begin a program of long-range strategic planning during the early 1980s.

Endnotes

1. *ASTR Newsletter*, Spring 1972, p. 1.
2. *ASTR Newsletter*, January 1973, p. 1.
3. Ibid., p. 3.
4. Ibid.
5. *ASTR Newsletter*, January 1974, p. 1.
6. *American Society for Therapeutic Radiologists Standing Committees for 1974–1975*, pp. 1–3.
7. *American Society for Therapeutic Radiologists Amendments to the Constitution and Bylaws*, Fall 1974, p. 1.
8. Digitally Recorded Oral History Interview with John Curry, Fairfax, Virginia, February 13, 2008, p. 5.
9. *ASTR Newsletter*, Fall 1974, p. 2.
10. *ASTR Newsletter*, August 2, 1976, pp. 1–3.
11. Frank R. Hendrickson, chairman, American Society for Therapeutic Radiologists, letter to the Office of Planning, Evaluation, and Legislation, Health Resources Administration, November 8, 1977, p. 2.
12. Ibid.
13. *ASTR Newsletter*, June 1978, p. 3.
14. Ibid., p. 1.
15. *ASTR Newsletter*, July 1979, p. 1.
16. Robert G. Parker to Martin Coleman, June 13, 2003, p. 2.
17. Ibid.
18. Bill Beck Tape-recorded Oral History Interview with Frances Glica, Philadelphia, Pennsylvania, November 6, 2006, p. 1.
19. Ibid., p. 2.
20. Digitally Recorded Telephone Oral History Interview with Kathy Thomas, Fairfax County, Virginia, February 12, 2008, p. 1.
21. Bill Beck Tape-recorded Oral History Interview with Frances Glica, Philadelphia, Pennsylvania, November 6, 2006, p. 3.
22. N. Suntharalingam, Comments to Author, March 1, 2008, p. 3.
23. Ibid.
24. Ibid.

ASTRO met at the Fontainbleau Hilton three times, in 1981, 1985, and 1990. ASTRO first went to the Miami Beach hotel in 1981 when the accident at the Kansas City Hyatt Hotel forced the society to move to another site.

CHAPTER NINE

ASTRO and Long-Range Planning

1982–1990

fter making great strides during the 1970s, the American Society of Therapeutic Radiologists (ASTR) started the 1980s with a stroke of bad luck that was unprecedented in the society's twenty-plus-year history. In early 1981, ASTR issued its "Call for Scientific Papers" for the society's twenty-third annual meeting, which was scheduled for the Hyatt Regency Hotel Crown Center in Kansas City in mid-October. The ASTR annual meeting would include sessions in joint sponsorship with the American Association of Physicists in Medicine (AAPM), the Radiation Research Society (RRS), and the American Society of Radiologic Technologists (ASRT).[1]

On July 17, 1981, more than 2,000 people were in the atrium of the recently completed Hyatt Regency Crown Center to attend a dance contest when a walkway on the fourth floor failed, crashed into the second floor walkway and plunged to the floor of the atrium below, killing 114 people and injuring more than 200.[2]

The Hyatt Regency tragedy and the closing of the Kansas City hotel was a personal blow to Jack Travis, the Topeka radiotherapist who served as ASTR president in 1979–1980. Fortunately, Travis, who described himself as the "first community/country radiotherapist" to hold the office of ASTR president, and the ASTR staff were able to line up a replacement hotel, the Fontainebleu in Miami Beach, on extremely short notice.[3] As it was, the Miami Beach meeting was one of the society's best meetings to that time and a healing experience given the circumstances.

The decade that started under such an ill-fated star would turn out to be a successful one, one that was characterized by several important changes. ASTR would confront the challenges of the future by establishing a tradition of long-range planning that would mark the organization for the next quarter-century. The society also would restructure its relationship with the American College of Radiology (ACR), signing a 1988 management contract with the ACR that would be renewed each year for the next ten years. ASTR's Board also authorized renaming of the society in 1983 as the American Society for Therapeutic Radiology and Oncology (ASTRO). Through all the changes of the 1980s, ASTRO would expand its membership, increase its revenues and extend its influence.

On July 17, 1981, a walkway collapsed at the Hyatt Crown Center Hotel, two months before ASTR was scheduled to meet at the Kansas City convention facility.

The Power of Planning

The idea of conducting long-range planning to give ASTR leaders the best set of data for decision-making in the future dated to the late 1970s. Seymour Levitt appointed ASTR's first Long-range Planning Committee during his tenure as president in 1979. Jack Travis, who succeeded Levitt as ASTR president, continued his predecessor's focus on planning and widened the approach to authorize the first comprehensive Membership Survey of the society since the days of the club in the late 1950s. The response was little short of phenomenal, with 52 percent of society members taking the time to complete the survey at a time when 10 to 15 percent response to similar surveys was considered excellent.[4]

The 1980 Membership Survey was intriguing for what it revealed about the composition of the society's membership. For one thing, members were quite a bit younger than the membership of other medical societies, such as the American Medical Association (AMA). A full 69 percent of ASTR's members were between the age of thirty-five and fifty-four, compared with just 46 percent of AMA members who were in the same age bracket.[5]

John W. Travis, president of ASTR in 1979–1980.

ASTR members also were more involved with universities than the average member of the AMA. Slightly more than three-quarters of the society's membership held a medical school appointment, but only one-third of the members were full-time faculty. Just over half of society members (53 percent) practiced in a community sector setting. Four of ten members practiced in one- or two-man groups, and 70 percent of members were in groups of four physicians or less. Still, more than 30 percent of the membership practiced in multispecialty groups of five or more. Almost 60 percent of the practices surveyed reported seeing between two hundred and four hundred new patients per physician per year.[6]

Unlike members surveyed in 1959, ASTR's members in 1980 were primarily products of US medical schools. Slightly more than seven in ten members (72.2 percent) of ASTR's members had received their training from medical schools in the United States, a complete change from the results of the survey twenty years before.[7]

Members' concerns were varied and specific. Fully three-quarters of the respondents worried about the availability of radiation therapy technologists. A shortage had been growing for more than a decade. The role of medical oncologists, and clinical research in combined surgery and chemotherapy were of increasing concern to the vast majority of members. Finally, nearly every member who responded to the survey cited government regulation and reimbursement policies as a concern.[8]

Samuel Hellman, president of ASTRO in 1982–1983.

ASTR's 1980 Membership Survey was a critical component of background material for the society's first five-year strategic plan late in 1981. Herman Suit was president when the survey was tabulated and the first strategic plan was completed. The plan was presented to the ASTR Board of Directors early in 1982, and it included a multitude of goals that would address the needs of members who had responded to the survey. "In doing this we are aware that we must develop new programs, strengthen current programs, and define those programs which can be developed with the cooperation and support of the American College of Radiology," William C. Johnson, chair of the Long-range Planning Committee, explained about the plan's next steps.[9]

Johnson and his Planning Committee had identified a number of immediate priorities for ASTR, including the recruitment and training of additional radiation therapy technologists; mechanisms to improve interaction with medical and surgical oncology; and ways to make the society more responsive to the myriad of government or third-party payer regulations, particularly relating to reimbursement, legislation, regulations, and cost containment.[10] Other immediate priorities included the education of radiation oncology trainees, the need to improve representation of membership on ASTR committees, the stabilization of ASTR finances by the adoption of accrual accounting, project-specific budgeting and the development of a reserve fund; and a review of current methods of recruitment that would allow ASTR to identify ways to provide manpower for the specialty, particularly physicians, radiation biologists, physicists, radiotherapy technologists, and dosimetrists.

That first long-range plan also foreshadowed what would be growing member dissatisfaction with the society's relationship with the ACR. Among the long-term priorities the plan intended to address were a number of intersociety issues, including communicating with the ACR about current and future dissatisfaction by ASTR members, improving the understanding by members of both societies about the joint services shared, and evaluating space needs for ASTR staff.[11]

Johnson and the Planning Committee recommended to the Board of Directors that it "focus on a few limited areas in order to best utilize staff, committee time, and limited financial resources."[12] The areas they recommended concentrating on were technologist training, the education of radiotherapy trainees, and stabilization of the society's finances, as well as establishing fund reserves.

No Man Is An Island

With its first long-range strategic plan in place, ASTR could look forward to its twenty-fourth annual meeting in Orlando in October 1982. As Carlos Perez handed the presidential gavel to Samuel Hellman, delegates to the record-setting annual meeting could take pride in the fact that radiotherapy was gaining new credibility in the fight against cancer. When *Reader's Digest* published an article titled "The Invisible Cancer Cure" in its April

1982 edition, the magazine brought the advances in radiotherapy to the attention of 100 million readers in a dozen languages worldwide. "Hundreds of thousands of people cured of cancer owe their lives to radiation," the magazine informed its readers.

What most readers didn't know was the role that ASTR played in preparation of that article. Walter Ross, the New York freelance writer who wrote the article, got the idea after reading a report in the nationally respected *Cancer Letter*, which had obtained its information from presentations by ASTR radiation oncologists at an ACR seminar for the media in Washington, DC, in the fall of 1981. It was a follow-up to a seminar that the ACR and ASTR had sponsored in New York City the previous year.[13]

The ASTR members who briefed the media at the trade press conference included Luther Brady, Morris Wizenberg. The topic discussed was organ preservation in breast cancer.

The media briefing increased awareness of radiation treatment options for those suffering from breast cancer. "There are many more telephone calls now from women seeking a second opinion with regards to their management (of breast cancer)," Brady said. "This number has risen dramatically with each effort in public relations beginning in October 1980 with publications relative to breast cancer management in *Ladies' Home Journal, Redbook, Harper's Bazaar*, and *Consumer Reports.*"[14]

It took outgoing president Carlos Perez to inject a bit of sobering reality into the enthusiasm that many in ASTR felt for the future of the society and the specialty. Perez, who would serve as the 1983 ASTR chairman, sounded a note of caution in his first Chairman's Report. "Notwithstanding that we represent a highly specialized group with specific areas of domain and skills, we must remember that we represent approximately ten percent of the membership of the American College of Radiology and less than one percent of the physicians in the United States."[15]

Perez titled his column "No Man Is an Island," and he meant it as a warning to his colleagues. "It is obvious that radiation oncology cannot function in a vacuum. We must relate closely not only to other oncological specialties but to the entire field of medicine and society in general," Perez said, referring to the difficulties radiation therapists sometimes had in interacting with their colleagues in medical oncology. "Over the past fifteen years, we have seen an increasing emphasis on high technology: the introduction of more sophisticated equipment, precision devices, and a great deal of computer applications in radiation oncology. Medical physicists and computer scientists have become our close associates, without whom it would be difficult to function in today's medical world. Radiation therapy technologists and nurses have contributed greatly to improve the care of the patient receiving cancer therapy, and we must make every effort to advance the professional education and position of these professionals within the oncological community."[16]

In short, Perez commanded his colleagues, "Let's get involved in the issues and get off the sidelines."[17]

One issue ASTR did get involved in was restructuring its relationship with the ACR. In February 1983, Sam Hellman, James Cox, Roy Deffebach, and Bill Moss met in San Diego with the Executive Committee of the Board of Chancellors of the American College of Radiology. They conveyed to the influential ACR members the "general dissatisfaction of ASTR members with our participation in college affairs and the desire for reorganization that would give us more voice and self determination."[18] ASTR and several of it committees would spend the next five years negotiating a more satisfactory management arrangement with the ACR.

A New Name

ASTR's search for independence took another step forward in 1983 when the Board of Directors ratified a membership desire for a new name to signify the increasing importance of radiation oncology. At the 1983 annual meeting in Los Angeles, the Board approved the change of the name to the American Society for Therapeutic Radiology and Oncology (ASTRO). Members had been lobbying since the early 1970s for a name that would reflect the society's growing identification with the practice of oncology.

In 1983, the ACR opened its headquarters in new offices in Reston, Virginia. John Curry moved to Reston, and Nick Croce stayed behind in the Philadelphia office, which continued to be responsible for ASTRO affairs.[19]

The pressure to gain more autonomy within the councils of the ACR also ramped up in the mid-1980s. For its part, the ACR took more notice of ASTRO and its interests. Otha Linton, ACR's Washington lobbyist, began writing a popular column in the *ASTRO Newsletter,* "Washington

Whispers," to explain the growing complexity of Washington regulatory initiatives aimed at the nation's healthcare communities. Linton's column during the period explained such concepts as diagnostis related groups (DRGs) and the Health Care Financing Agency (HCFA) and how they impacted the practice of radiation oncology.[20]

Matters with the ACR came to a head at the May 1984 ASTRO Board meeting when Sam Hellman reviewed the background of the relations between the two organizations that led to a proposal to form a joint ad hoc committee to discuss ASTRO's concerns. "There was no substantive impetus for change" in the position of the ACR Board. Consequently, the ASTRO Board voted to form the ad hoc committee to "investigate alternative organizational structures if the problems addressed by ASTRO are not adequately addressed by the ACR."[21]

Sarah Donaldson with Nick Croce, executive director of ASTRO from 1987 to 1995.

ASTRO met at the Westin Bonaventure Hotel in Los Angeles in 1983 and again in 1986.

Eric Hall and Bill Shipley with their spouses at an ASTRO reception in the 1980s.

Simon Kramer, the committee chairman, identified two items that he called essential to ensure adequate ASTRO representation within the ACR Council structure. Kramer pointed out that a radiation oncologist elected by radiation oncologists needed to sit on the ACR Executive Committee, and the ACR should immediately appoint a radiation oncologist to its Finance Committee.[22] Kramer, who had enjoyed a good working relationship with the ACR's John Curry for almost twenty years, was hesitant about establishing an independent presence for ASTRO.[23]

The fact that the Board of Directors could consider going it alone as a society separate from ACR management was a tribute to the work of James D. Cox, ASTRO's treasurer, and his colleagues on the Finance Committee. At the end of 1981, ASTR was deep in debt, with nearly $60,000 in red ink on its books.[24] In 1982, Cox and his finance team began making plans that would make the society self-sufficient within two years.[25]

ASTR raised dues to $125 a year in 1982 and wrote off more than $30,000 in past due and uncollectible dues receivables.[26] Cox became ASTRO's version of "Dr. No." He worked with the ACR's treasurer to untangle ASTRO's books from those of ACR and put ASTRO on an austere budget. "We also helped wipe out debt from 1982 to 1985 by being frugal," he said. "Back then, we had a lot of proposals for socioeconomic projects. I told people ASTRO couldn't afford them. They just tended to chew up the revenues."[27]

The society also raised the fees for exhibitors at its annual meetings. In 1983 and 1984, the annual meetings in Orlando and Los Angeles each brought in more than $100,000 excess of income over expense.[28] Pergamon, the publisher of the Red Journal, increased its minimum guarantee to the

James Cox, Luther Brady, and Bob Edland conferring during an ASTRO meeting in the 1980s.

society from $50,000 a year in 1983 to $65,000 in 1984.[29] Several large gifts also helped to defray ASTRO's expenses in 1983 and 1984.

As a result, Cox and the Finance Committee were able to report that the society was on solid financial footing by the time of the spring meeting of the ASTRO Board in May 1984. Cox noted that ASTRO's permanent reserve had been built to $85,000, with plans to add $115,000 to the reserve in 1984. Cox reported that ASTRO had more than $350,000 invested in short-term money market funds that had been returning 9 to 16 percent a year since 1980, and that the $40,000 in accounts payable left the society with a working margin of $310,000.[30]

Gerrald Hanks passing the gavel to Ted Phillips in 1984.

"This organization has achieved this financial stature by adherence to a firm budgeting policy, adoption of the Long-range Plan and a watchful eye on expenditures and revenues," Cox wrote.[31] The strong financial footing also was due to the dues increase, the income from the Red Journal and an increased number of exhibits at the annual scientific meeting. From the mid-1980s on, the exhibits underwrote the cost of the annual meeting while dues and subscription income supported the rest of the society's activities.

The Second Strategic Plan

A measure of the maturation of ASTRO came in 1986 during the presidency of James D. Cox when the society completed the second survey of its members and embarked on an updating of the five-year plan first unveiled in 1982. This time, member concern gravitated to specific issues. ASTRO conducted the survey by mailing it to a random sample of 25 percent of the membership. Nearly eight in ten members surveyed responded, an astonishing rate of 78 percent.

Respondents reported that they were worried about radiation oncology's lack of positive image among other physicians and the public, and a possible oversupply of radiation oncologists. That being said, respondents said they wanted ASTRO to make a priority of teaching radiation oncology to medical students. Also high on respondent's lists were ASTRO support of a quality assessment program and direct support of radiation oncology research.[32]

James Cox, president of ASTRO in 1985–1986.

ASTRO took quick action on the immediate priorities. In the spring of 1987, ASTRO Chairman James Cox announced the establishment of ASTRO fellowships for radiation oncology residents. "For the last several years," Cox noted, "members of the society and the Board of Directors have been gravely and increasingly concerned about a manpower crisis in academic radiation oncology. The demands on one's time, the energy required and the compensation received have measured poorly in the short run compared to a private practice career. This has led to a dramatic flight from academia of large numbers of junior and even senior faculty."[33]

Robert W. Edland, president of ASTRO in 1986–1987.

The ASTRO fellowships were funded through a variety of mechanisms, including interest income, implementation of a voluntary $100 annual dues supplement, and tax-deductible donations. Although not directly related to solving the manpower crisis in academia, the fellowship program did expose a new generation of radiation oncologists to the possibility of a career in academic medicine.

The quick establishment of the ASTRO fellowship program confirmed the value of the society's long-range planning efforts. Within a year's time, ASTRO had identified a major concern from the Membership Survey, evaluated solutions and costs, and addressed the problem.

The longstanding rift between ASTRO and the ACR also was settled to the satisfaction of both sides during the late 1980s. In September 1988, the Executive Council of the American College of Radiology devoted its entire meeting to the needs of its radiation oncology members. The Council supported the concept that qualified radiation oncology centers, whether publicly or privately financed, be treated equally by third-party carriers. The Council endorsed the Committee for Radition Oncology Blue Book recommendations contained in "Radiation Oncology in Integrated Cancer

Stanley Order passing the gavel to Carl R. Bogardus in 1989.

Management" of November 1986 pertaining to the establishment of guidelines for staff, including physicians, physicists, and dosimetrists, as well as equipment in radiation oncology facilities.

The ACR redefined the term *radiation oncologist* to the satisfaction of ASTRO, using the term to replace what many ASTRO members felt was an outdated term, *therapeutic radiologist*. The ACR pledged to develop lines of communication between its staff and representatives of other groups concerned with radiation oncology, including federal agencies and manufacturers of radiation therapy equipment. Finally, the Council approved a resolution stipulating that a responsible physician be available for consultation and supervision, either on the premises or nearby, when patients are receiving radiation treatment—a Health Care Financing Agency requirement.[34]

"The American College of Radiology has been extremely cooperative and responsive to the needs of physicians practicing radiation oncology and has committed considerable resources of the College to the efforts of radiation oncology, especially in the socio-economic area," ASTRO Chairman Robert Edland told members in his column in the *ASTRO Newsletter.*[35]

So the society seemed to be satisfied with the ACR's increased attention to the needs of its radiation oncology members. This was reflected by ASTRO's decision to approve a 1988 management services contract with the college. The $140,000 annual contract provided for all administrative and support services, and included 80 percent of the salary of Nick Croce, the executive director; 80 percent of the salary of Frances Glica, the office secretary; and 70 percent of the salary of an ACR meeting planner in the Chicago office.[36] The revised agreement, renewable annually, would continue in force for the next decade.

ASTRO as an organization, and radiation oncology as a practice, both expanded their influence during the 1980s. Thanks to its attention to long-range planning and budgeting, ASTRO laid the foundation for the continuing strong growth the society would experience during the 1990s.

Endnotes

1. "Call for Scientific Papers," *Twenty-third Annual Scientific Meeting of the American Society of Therapeutic Radiologists*, 1981, pp. 1–4.

2. "Hyatt Regency Walkway Collapse," www.en.wikipedia.org/wiki/Hyatt_Regency_Walkway_Collapse

3. John W. Travis, Topeka, Kansas, Letter to Martin Coleman, Fairfax, Virginia, July 15, 2003, p. 1.

4. "Long-range Planning Committee Report," *ASTR Newsletter,* vol. I, no. I, Spring 1982, p. 5.

5. *ASTR Membership Survey*, 1980, p. 2.

6. Ibid.

7. Ibid., p. 1.

8. Ibid., p. 4.

9. "Long-range Planning Committee Report," *ASTR Newsletter,* vol. 1, no. 2, 1982, p. 6.

10. Ibid.

11. Ibid.

12. Ibid.

13. Charles Honaker, "Report on Public Relations," *ASTR Newsletter,* vol. 1, no. 2, 1982, p. 6.

14. Ibid., p. 7.

15. Carlos A. Perez, "Chairman's Report," *ASTR Newsletter,* vol. 1, no. 3, 1982, p. 1.

16. Ibid., p. 2.

17. Ibid.

18. Carlos A. Perez, "Chairman's Report," *ASTR Newsletter,* vol. 1, no. 4, 1983, p. 2.

19. Digitally Recorded Oral History Interview with John Curry, Fairfax, Virginia, February 13, 2008, p. 3.

20. Otha Linton, Washington Whispers, *ASTRO Newsletter,* vol. II, no. 3, 1983, p. 5.

21. "ASTRO/ACR Relationship," *ASTRO Board Meeting Minutes*, May 16, 1984, American College of Radiology, Philadelphia, p. 4.

22. Ibid., p. 4.

23. Digitally Recorded Oral History Interview with John Curry, Fairfax, Virginia, February 13, 2008, p. 3.

24. James D. Cox, *Treasurer's Report and Analysis of Reserves*, May 14, 1984, p. 1.

25. "Report of the ASTR Treasurer," *Minutes of American Society for Therapeutic Radiologists Board of Directors*, Philadelphia, Pennsylvania, May 12, 1982, p. 1.

26. Ibid.

27. Interview with James D. Cox, p. 4.

28. Annual Meeting, Los Angeles, 1984, *Report of the ASTRO Treasurer*, p. 1.

29. "Society Journal," *American Society for Therapeutic Radiology and Oncology Board Meeting Minutes*, Philadelphia, Pennsylvania, May 16, 1984, p. 3.

30. James D. Cox, *Treasurer's Report and Analysis of Reserves*, May 14, 1984, Appendix II.

31. Ibid.

32. Hywel-Madoc Jones, "Report of Long-range Planning Committee—1986 Membership Survey," *ASTRO Newsletter,* vol. V, no. 1, 1986, p. 2.

33. James D. Cox, "Chairman's Report," *ASTRO Newsletter,* vol. V, no. 2, 1987, p. 1.

34. Robert Edland, "Chairman's Report: ACR Council Actions Impact Radiation Oncology," *ASTRO Newsletter,* vol. VI, no. 1, 1988, pp. 1, 6.

35. Ibid., p. 6.

36. "Memo," *ACR/ASTRO Management Services Agreement*, December 3, 1987, pp. 1–9.

Rodney Million, president 1990–1991; Phil Rubin, president 1977–1978; and Florence Chu at one of the ASTRO business meetings.

CHAPTER TEN

ASTRO in the 1990s

1991–1998

The 1990s were very good years for ASTRO and radiation therapy. ASTRO began the decade with two thousand members, and it tripled its membership to six thousand members by the dawn of the twenty-first century. The society became increasingly involved in socioeconomic issues, often representing the interests of its members in such disparate legislative and regulatory initiatives as compensation inequities and the regulation of medical radioactive waste.

Like most of the rest of the nation's medical community, ASTRO was affected by the healthcare changes of the era, especially the impact of health maintenance organizations (HMOs) and provider payment organizations (PPOs) for radiation oncology services.

The society took advantage of new technologies when it began to make effective use of desktop computers, which became much more sophisticated and powerful during the 1990s. The spread of the Internet during the 1990s allowed ASTRO to create and expand a Web site as well as to enhance communication to its members and constituents through frequent e-mail messages, listserves, and electronic newsgroups.

There was a tremendous upsurge in medical technology in the 1990s as well, particularly in the radiological specialties as diagnostic radiologists developed more sophisticated ways of determining the extent of the cancer, and radiation oncologists developed more sophisticated ways of delivering radiation to the target area.

In diagnostic radiology, the introduction of fast, multislice computed tomography (CT) scanners, new magnetic resonance imaging (MRI) techniques, metabolic imaging with position emission tomography (PET) scanning, and machines that fused PET and CT images made it possible to determine more precisely the extent of the tumor and critical normal tissues. In radiation oncology, the development of three-dimensional treatment planning, intensity modulated radiation therapy, tomotherapy and stereotactic radiosurgery made it possible to deliver higher doses of radiation to the tumor with less dose to intervening normal tissues. These advances revolutionized treatment planning and offered a better chance for local tumor control and lower complication rates.

ASTRO underwent significant changes in its educational program during this period, too, including changes in the curriculum at the annual meeting and, for the first time, offering a number of smaller scientific and educational programs throughout the year.

J. Frank Wilson, president of ASTRO in 1992–1993 and the society's unofficial historian.

Changes in the Structures of the Educational Program

The 1980s and 1990s also brought significant changes to the ASTRO meeting structure. ASTRO enjoyed spectacular growth of its annual meetings during the 1990s, providing members with hundreds of scientific sessions, refresher courses, topical seminars, and panel discussions held as part of the annual meeting.

One of the first new features was the Meet the Professor Luncheon, which began in 1984 during Ted Phillips' presidency. In this session, residents have an opportunity have lunch with prominent faculty members from around the globe and discuss issues of interest to the residents. The luncheon harkened back to the 1970s when Juan del Regato, Gilbert Fletcher, and others would pull up a lawn chair at an annual meeting and reminisce about the early days of radiation therapy. The presidential address, started in 1988 by Stanley E. Order, was a forty-five-minute address by the president on the subject of his choice.

Rodney Million was chair in 1991 and Sarah Donaldson was president when ASTRO established the first plenary session at the society's annual scientific meeting. The plenary session created an opportunity for the

Kathy Thomas, longtime ASTRO staff liaison for education.

Rodney R. Million, ASTRO president in 1990–1991, and Sarah S. Donaldson, ASTRO president in 1991–1992.

David Hussey, Steve Leibel, Sarah Donaldson, Lester Peters, Rodney Million, and Frank Wilson at an ASTRO meeting.

Ritsuko Komaki served as chair of ASTRO's Education Committee during much of the 1990s.

Marvin Z. Rotman, who wrote ASTRO's Code of Ethics in the 1990s.

presentation of some of the most important papers at the annual meeting. The plenary sessions are unopposed, with no competing lectures or refresher courses to divert the attention of attendees. The plenary sessions highlighted the presentation of what became known as "practice changing" papers.

ASTRO enhanced its outreach activities to foster leadership growth in the society during the decade by establishing a Young Members Group that was comprised of members in their first five years of practice.

J. Frank Wilson was president and Sarah Donaldson was chair in 1992 when another major change took place. For the first time in ASTRO's history that year, the society's annual meeting was too big to be held in a hotel. The meeting was held in the San Diego Convention Center that year, and it has been held in a convention center every year since.

Another landmark year for the ASTRO annual scientific meeting was 1995. Since it was the centennial of Roentgen's discovery of X-rays, the meeting included a major historical lecture. That was one of the years in which the ASTRO Board experimented with debates at the meeting, and Jay Harris, the 1995 president, instituted the president's categorical course as well as poster discussion sessions.

Several changes came about in 1998 and 1999. David Hussey, president-elect, chaired the first past-president's breakfast at the annual meeting that year, a session designed to accomplish two things: make past leaders aware of issues affecting the society and to provide current leaders the opportunity to benefit from the knowledge and experience of prior leaders. That same year, Christopher Rose initiated a meeting of the leadership and the exhibitors to share ideas about how to improve the exhibits. The meeting with exhibitors has been held annually since then. The Socioeconomic Luncheon, the first to be held by the society, was begun in 1998 and continues to bring experts in the field together to provide information about socioeconomic issues and answer questions from members.

At the urging of Eli Glatstein, another significant change dating back to Lester Peters' presidency was the introduction of contested elections. Prior to 1992, the Nominating Committee selected a slate of officers that was then voted in by the membership at the annual meeting. The debate over contested elections was a contentious one, which continues even today.

Who Represents Radiation Oncologists?

Carl R. "Bob" Bogardus, ASTRO president in 1990, identified an issue for the society that had been of concern to ASTRO leadership for several years. "Have we given up being a sideline of diagnostic radiology only to become a sideline of medical oncology?" Bogardus asked in his column in the *ASTRO Newsletter* in the spring of 1990.[1]

Eli Glatstein, who suggested that ASTRO hold contested elections for its officers.

Bogardus noted that ASTRO members should never forget "the enormous effort that has gone into developing radiation oncology as a freestanding specialty equal or superior to others in the treatment of patients with malignancy. Cooperative and concomitant treatment is acceptable and desirable. We should treat our colleagues as equals, expect to be treated in the same manner, and steadfastly refuse employment by, and hence subservience to others."[2]

Commenting on the growth of the American Society of Clinical Oncology (ASCO) and its claims to the American Medical Association that it had a greater number of radiation oncologists than any other medical specialty organization, Bogardus noted "the mission of ASCO is totally different from the mission of ASTRO. In spite of the fact that we are fifteen percent of the ASCO membership, we do not have any representation on the Board of ASCO, nor do we chair any ASCO Committee."[3]

Stanley E. Order, ASTRO's 1990 chairman, urged all radiation oncologists to participate in ASTRO and the American College of Radiology (ACR), if they wanted the practice to have a strong voice in matters concerning the specialty. If they didn't participate, Order said, "I assure you others will represent you, and represent you inadequately."[4]

Carl R. Bogardus, president of ASTRO in 1989–1990.

ASTRO waged another battle in the jurisdictional war to represent radiation oncology during the 1990s, and that was with the American College of Radiation Oncology (ACRO). In 1990 a group of radiation oncologists led by Luther Brady decided to form a separate college, ACRO, in order to secure more representation for radiation oncology, especially in the area of socioeconomics.[5]

Steven A. Leibel, 1996 ASTRO president, recalled that "there was some opposition to putting a focus on socioeconomic issues. ACRO was formed to address the same issues that were brought up to the American College of Radiology at the time. ACRO pointed out that ACR didn't speak for radiation oncology."[6]

During the 1980s and 1990s, as radiation oncology was becoming established as a distinct specialty, radiation oncologists began to feel that their interests were not being well represented by the ACR. This was before ASTRO was willing to take on the responsibility. There was talk during the 1980s about "lobbying being very expensive," and that "radiation oncology was too small a specialty" to have a voice in dealings with the Health Care

Financing Agency (HCFA), the agency responsible for Medicare oversight. Others in ASTRO argued equally as eloquently that radiation oncology was lacking a voice at the socioeconomic table. As a result, many radiation oncologists weren't happy with the arrangement.

There were strong advocates for ACRO (Luther Brady) and strong advocates for the ACR (J. Frank Wilson), but there were also a growing number of people who would like to see ASTRO take the lead in matters dealing with socioeconomic and government affairs. Many of those in ASTRO leadership positions felt that eventually ASTRO would be the only radiation oncology society dealing with socioeconomic issues, but most don't think that is the case yet, in spite of the fact that the latest strategic plan (2001) stated that ASTRO was to be "the voice for radiation oncology."

The specialty also had to deal with other turf issues during this period. One was with neurosurgery. In 1991, David Larson pointed out to ASTRO leadership that a radiosurgery turf war was brewing between members of ASTRO and members of the American Association of Neurological Surgeons (AANS). Radiation oncologists and neurosurgeons both thought that the emerging field of brain radiosurgery was rightfully theirs.

Larson suggested ASTRO create a task force to make recommendations on the increasingly thorny problem. This task force, which Larson chaired, found that AANS also had formed its own competing task force. "In 1993," Larson said, "I contacted the AANS/CNS task force leaders and suggested that we join forces and produce a mutually acceptable document to define radiosurgery, what it requires and who performs it."[7]

The cooperation resulted in the publication of an identical article in the leading journal of each specialty. The article set the standard of care for brain radiosurgery in the United States and showed that radiation oncologists, neurosurgeons and physicists all make important contributions for successful radiosurgery.

ASTRO's Strategic Planning Initiatives

During the 1990s, ASTRO continued the strategic planning it had begun the previous decade with strategic plans in 1980 and again in 1986. ASTRO Chair Sarah Donaldson convened the decade's first strategic planning retreat at the American College of Radiology (ACR) headquarters in Reston, Virginia, in 1993. The purpose, Donaldson explained, "was to review ASTRO's past and future role in radiation oncology."[8]

Donaldson opened her presentation by noting that ASTRO had become the largest society of radiation oncologists in the world with an active membership of more than twenty-eight hundred. "Ninety-five percent of board certified radiation oncologists are members of ASTRO," Donaldson reported. "This represents a strong volunteer base from which ASTRO can draw on to meet the goals of the society."[9]

The most visible activity was the society's annual scientific meeting. ASTRO was on financially sound ground, and it had not increased

membership dues since the early 1980s. ASTRO had great strengths, Donaldson said, but it also had weaknesses that it needed to address. "The society," she said, "had not been proactive in meeting the challenges of the technological and socioeconomic forces which have emerged over the past several years."[10] ASTRO's governance structure had remained essentially the same for thirty-five years, resulting in the perception among some members of "an old boys' network" more interested in limiting participation in the society's affairs than in serving its members.

A number of recommendations emanated from the retreat. First and foremost, the ASTRO Board recommended that the society clearly define its role in socioeconomic matters. Board members agreed that ASTRO should be involved in legislative affairs affecting health policy issues, including reimbursement. Other recommendations from the retreat were that ASTRO continue its longtime relationship with the Council of Affiliated Regional Radiation Oncology Societies (CARROS) and encourage membership of physicists and biologists. The Board agreed to waive the application fee and first-year dues for prospective radiobiologists and radiation physicist members.[11] The Board also recommended the creation of a number of new committees to deal with the rapidly changing health-care environment.[12]

The Search for Self-representation

ASTRO revisited its strategic planning initiative in 1997 when Board Chair Steven Leibel initiated a revision of the strategic plan recommendations that came out of the Reston retreat in 1993. Leibel, who had spent six years chairing ASTRO's Scientific Program Committee, assembled his Strategic Planning Committee early in 1997 and made a presentation to the Board of Directors in late summer.

Leibel's committee surveyed the ASTRO membership to get their input on where the society should be headed in the coming five years. Not surprisingly, most members were happy with ASTRO for its scientific and educational programs. "However," Leibel said, "it is also clear that our members want ASTRO to deal with issues that are beyond its current mission," including influencing third-party payers, affecting federal govern-

Michael L. Steinberg, chair of ASTRO's Economics Committee in the 1990s.

ment policy, and reducing the oversupply of radiation oncologists.[13] The strategic plan changed the mission statement to define ASTRO as the key organization "representing radiation oncology in a rapidly evolving socio-economic healthcare environment."[14]

The 1997 strategic plan that followed listed a series of goals. Primary among them was the goal of positioning ASTRO to become the "voice of radiation oncology." Implementation of the strategic plan required action items such as restructuring the staff, hiring an executive director, forming a Government Relations Committee and establishing socioeconomic goals.

The emerging strategic plan was laid out to broaden ASTRO's mission to include socioeconomic concerns; to expand government relations activities; and to monitor new technologies and assess them through consensus statement development. To achieve these goals, the committee proposed a summit of radiation oncology organizations to clarify roles in light of ASTRO's new mission.[15]

Related objectives included establishing an ASTRO Practice Guidelines Group, strengthening the relationship between ASTRO and CAR-ROS, expanding ASTRO's international activities, and strengthening the National Cancer Institute's intramural and extramural radiation oncology programs.[16]

Socioeconomic Issues

From the time Ronald Reagan moved into the White House in 1981, Congress and the administration ramped up an interjection of politics into the healthcare debate that had begun with the administration of Lyndon B. Johnson in the mid-1960s. Government regulation of healthcare took center stage in 1992 and 1993 when First Lady Hillary Clinton attempted to revamp the nation's health insurance system. Radiation oncologists, along with the rest of the nation's medical community, were subjected to reams of regulations as politicians attempted to rein in spiraling healthcare costs.

ASTRO and its members went from dealing with Blue Cross/Blue Shield health insurance plans to serving patients enrolled in health maintenance organizations (HMOs) and provider payment organizations (PPOs). Radiation oncologists learned a whole new set of compensation acronyms, including DRGs (diagnosis related groups) and RVUs (relative value units).

Because of ASTRO's management contract with the American College of Radiology, much of the society's socioeconomic initiatives were coordinated by the ACR, although the negotiation of the 1988 management contract had resulted in the ACR opening its governance to increased representation for radiation oncologists. Carlos Perez, ASTRO's representative to the ACR Council, reported in 1991 that there were now three radiation oncologists on the ACR Board of Chancellors, a significant change from just three years before when there were no radiation oncologists on the Board of Chancellors.[17]

Stanley Order, the society's immediate past-chairman, identified the problem that ASTRO and its members faced early in the 1990s. Against the background of a proliferation of specialty medical organizations representing different components of radiation oncology, and the fight that ASTRO had been waging with the American College of Radiation Oncology (ACRO) for membership and influence, Order wrote, "HCFA, Medicare, Congress and industry are collectively trying to reduce medical care cost by reducing the future reimbursement in the treatment of cancer patients."[18]

But even with the ACR going to bat for its radiation oncology members, grassroots ASTRO sentiment was increasingly in favor of ASTRO taking an activist role on socioeconomic issues. Gerald E. Hanks was a leader of the ASTRO faction most vocal in its opposition to ACRO's attempts to represent the specialty of radiation oncology in the increasingly complex socioeconomic arena. Hanks argued that the formation of the ASTRO Federal Legislative Oversight Committee and the establishment of the ACR/ASTRO radiation oncology and government relations partnership were concrete steps to help ASTRO make the transition from a purely scientific society to one that was able to represent its members' interests in multiple forums.[19]

In the 1990s, the society abandoned its longtime policy of not getting involved with socioeconomic issues. "The majority of the membership, if given their preference," ASTRO Chairman Carl Bogardus explained in 1990, "would choose to take care of their patients, to be adequately reimbursed for their efforts, and to allow someone else to deal with the socioeconomic issues. Historically, ASTRO as an organization had maintained this posture."[20]

Socioeconomic and compensation issues would continue to be important components of ASTRO's agenda for the remainder of the 1990s. The issue of healthcare costs would come into even sharper focus between 1992 and 1994 when President Bill Clinton made healthcare reform one of the cornerstones of his administration.

Too Many Radiation Oncologists

For ASTRO a trend that was first identified in the early 1990s would become one of the thorniest issues the society would face during the decade. For much of its history since the 1950s, radiation oncology had been a specialty that was characterized by manpower shortages. But the glamour of society's war against cancer and a substantial increase in interest in careers in radiation oncology by medical students had turned the shortages around by 1990.

Even though there were slightly fewer training programs for radiation oncologists after the early 1980s, the number of full-time practitioners continued to climb during the decade. By 1990, the Education Commission of the ACR Committee on Radiation Oncology predicted a surplus of radiation oncologists. The actual number of radiation oncologists entering practice in 1990 versus the number of those retiring each year created a surplus of 550 radiation oncologists nationwide that year.[21]

For ASTRO, the growing number of radiation oncologists constituted a double-edged sword. On the one hand, radiation oncologists were all

Lester J. Peters, president of ASTRO in 1993–1994.

candidates for membership in the society. But at a time when government cost control measures were creating compensation issues for radiation oncologists and other physicians, the growth of the specialty created undeniable stresses within ASTRO.

Active membership in ASTRO climbed from just over two thousand in 1990 to thirty-three hundred in 1995.[22] The near 50 percent growth in five years allowed ASTRO to increase its revenues and put its finances on a sound footing for further growth in the 1990s. However, the growth of the specialty clearly concerned many members. By 1994, estimates were that the surplus of radiation oncologists was actually growing. Figures that year indicated that 165 radiation oncologists had entered practice in the United States; only forty-five radiation oncologists retired from practice that year.[23]

The absolute growth in the number of radiation oncologists wasn't across all segments of the radiation oncology community, however. Sarah S. Donaldson, ASTRO's 1992 president, reported that, "while we now observe an oversupply of radiation oncologists in the United States, we simultaneously face a lack of trainees and young radiation oncologists entering the academic arena."[24]

The problem bedeviled ASTRO for most of the decade. Members complained that the oversupply, coupled with the federal squeeze on healthcare costs, was costing them money. But truth be told, there was little ASTRO could do about the oversupply issue. From a legal standpoint, ASTRO would be subject to antitrust litigation on restraint of trade grounds if it actively attempted to restrict the number of residents entering the field.[25] ASTRO's role in the crisis was limited to data collection and statistical analyses, dissemination of information about the oversupply of radiation oncologists, establishment of employment clearinghouses and legislative strategies.

In the end, the oversupply of radiation oncologists did not turn out to be as big a problem as ASTRO had thought. The general population was growing and aging, and therefore, there were more cancer patients to treat. New indications were being developed for the use of radiotherapy. Some of newer techniques, such as Intensity Modulated Radiation Therapy (IMRT), required more hours of work from radiation oncologists, physicists, and dosimetrists, and radiation therapy facilities continued to be developed in cities that did not have them before. Before long the number of people retiring from the profession would increase, while the number of new trainees would remain fairly constant.

Information Technology

One technology tool that ASTRO was able to utilize to meet a number of its strategic planning goals was the Internet. With the *International Journal of Radiation Oncology*Biology*Physics,* ASTRO became the scientific voice of radiation oncology. A 1994 agreement between ASTRO and Pergamon/ Elsevier, the publishers of the Red Journal, ensured that the publication would remain the voice of ASTRO for years to come.[26]

But the sheer ability to reach millions of people online meant ASTRO could communicate its positions to internal and external audiences. In 1997, Chris Rose, the chair of ASTRO's Communications and Public Policy Committee, accepted the assignment of establishing an ASTRO presence on the Web. Assisted by Brian Goldsmith of Walter Reed Army Medical Center and Prabhakar Tripuraneni, the chief of radiation oncology at the Scripps Clinic and Research Foundation, the committee unveiled www.astro.org in 1998.[27]

"We also hope to use the board for electronic commerce," Rose wrote in the summer of 1997. "The Committee is aware of all sorts of interesting patient education materials, tumor board slide sets, oncology compendia, etc., that have been locally produced. We hope to create an 'electronic bazaar' where these materials might be made available and downloadable inexpensively."[28]

ASTRO's planning and preparation during the 1990s for the twenty-first century allowed the society to consider one of the most momentous changes in its history. In 1998, ASTRO made a step it had been contemplating for years when it severed its management agreement with the American College of Radiology and embarked upon the path of self-management.

Endnotes

1. Carl R. Bogardus, "President's Corner," *ASTRO Newsletter,* Spring 1990, p. 3.

2. Ibid.

3. Ibid.

4. Stanley E. Order, "Chairman's Report," *ASTRO Newsletter,* Spring 1990, p. 4.

5. David Larson e-mail to David Hussey, December 12, 2007.

6. Tape-recorded Oral History Interview with Steven A. Leibel, Philadelphia, Pennsylvania, November 10, 2006, p. 3.

7. David Larson e-mail to David Hussey, January 8, 2008, p. 1.

8. "To ASTRO Members from the ASTRO Board of Directors," Special Report, *ASTRO Newsletter*, September 1993, p. 1.

9. "Strengths," Special Report, *ASTRO Newsletter*, September 1993, p. 2.

10. "Weaknesses," Special Report, *ASTRO Newsletter*, September 1993, p. 3.

11. "Recommendation," Special Report, *ASTRO Newsletter*, September 1993, p. 6.

12. Ibid., pp. 4–5.

13. Ibid., p. 1.

14. Ibid.

15. Steven A. Leibel, *ASTRO's Strategic Plan*, Special Chairman's Report, August 1997, p. 1.

16. Ibid., p. 1.

17. Carlos Perez, "Report of ACR Councilor," *ASTRO Newsletter,* Fall/Winter 1990, p. 4.

18. Stanley Order, "Disunited We Fall," *ASTRO Newsletter,* Fall/Winter 1990, p. 6.

19. Gerald E. Hanks, "Working together instead of against one another," *ASTRO Newsletter,* Summer 1991, p. 3.

20. Carl R. Bogardus, "Chairman's Report," *ASTRO Newsletter,* Fall/Winter 1990, p. 1.

21. Ibid., p. 4.

22. "Active Membership in ASTRO," *ASTRO Newsletter,* Special Edition, April 1996, p. 7.

23. "Is There an Oversupply of Radiation Oncologists?," *ASTRO Newsletter,* Special Edition, April 1996, p. 5.

24. Sarah S. Donaldson, "President's Corner: The Support of Scholarship—A Societal Responsibility," *ASTRO Newsletter,* Fall/Winter 1991, p. 2.

25. "Legal Consequences," *ASTRO Newsletter,* Special Edition, April 1996, p. 4.

26. J. Frank Wilson, "Chairman's Report," *ASTRO Newsletter,* Summer 1994, p. 1.

27. Chris Rose, "ASTRO Communications and Public Policy News," *ASTRO Newsletter,* August 1997, p. 4.

28. Ibid.

Theodore Lawrence, ASTRO president in 2003–2004, moderates a poster discussion session.

CHAPTER ELEVEN

ASTRO in a New Century

1999–2008

ASTRO embarked on a new century in 2000 with high hopes. The society had taken control of its own destiny in the late 1990s when Steven Leibel, Richard Hoppe, Larry Kun, and Christopher Rose, ASTRO's leadership from 1995 to 2000, negotiated an amicable split with the American College of Radiology. ASTRO's decision to embrace self-management came in the wake of a strategic planning initiative that stressed the society's desire to achieve management independence. ASTRO greeted the new millennium with leased offices in Fairfax, Virginia, and a recognition on the part of ASTRO leadership that independence would guide the society's future in the twenty-first century.

Meeting Innovations

ASTRO introduced a multitude of meeting innovations in the decade between 1995 and 2005. The new initiative started with Jay Harris' introduction of the president's categorical course in 1995. This is typically a full-day course that is held on the day before the annual scientific meeting opens. It is a categorical course organized by the president on a focused topic of his or her choice.

Poster discussion sessions also started in 1995. These are sessions in which assigned reviewers summarize and lead the discussion of posters in his or her areas of expertise. The authors of the posters are available to answer questions about their work.

In 1997, ASTRO started having socioeconomic luncheons. Richard Hoppe was president that year, and Steve Leibel was chairman. These were conceived as sessions given by members who are experts in the socioeconomic aspects of practice. Over the years, that has included Carl Bogardus, Ted "Jerry" Brickner, Chris Rose, Mike Steinberg, Paul Wallner, and many others.[1]

In 1999, ASTRO began to have a special program for oncology nurses. That was also the first year for handing out refresher course syllabi for *all* of the refresher courses to all attendees. Prior to that time, each refresher course director would give a syllabus for his/her course to only those who attended that course.

The new century spawned a host of innovative changes for ASTRO's annual scientific meetings. In 2000, during Christopher Rose's chairmanship, ASTRO instituted the now very popular audience interactive sessions. The audience is asked to respond to presenters' questions by keying in a response on hand-held remotes, and results were displayed graphically to the audience within a few seconds.

"One of the concerns I've had with national meetings is that they aren't the most effective means of educating people," said David Hussey, who was a member of the ASTRO Executive Committee when interactive sessions were introduced. "I was on the ABR [American Board of Radiology] at the time, and I polled a number of leading radiation oncology educators, asking them to rank a variety of educational venues, such as national meetings, regional meetings, focused meetings, journals, textbooks, one-on-one teaching debates and the like. National meetings came out pretty low as a means of educating people. The problem is that it's an 'in one ear and out the other' experience."[2]

Hussey said his research pointed out the "need to get the audience involved. That's why debates are much better learning experiences than lectures, and focused meetings such as workshops are better at transferring knowledge than general meetings covering a wide variety of topics. So when the technology came along allowing us to ask the audience to respond to questions during the lecture, we looked upon it as a big step forward."[3]

That same year, the scientific sessions began hosting "NCI Listens" sessions in which representatives of the National Cancer Institute fielded questions from the radiotherapy community. In 2002, President Nora Janjan presided over the first annual scientific meeting in which webcasts of parts of the program were made available for download on members' PDAs, an initiative that had been championed by 2004–2005 President Prabhakar Tripuraneni. "This gave radiation oncologists who weren't able to attend the meeting an opportunity to view some of the most important parts of the meeting," Hussey said. "It also allowed attendees to evaluate the meeting and register online for CME credits."[4]

Christopher M. Rose, president of ASTRO in 1998–1999.

Allen Lichter delivering a plenary session address.

David H. Hussey, ASTRO president in 1999–2000.

In 2003, ASTRO introduced the Survivor Circle, a place where cancer survivors' pictures and stories are displayed. It's a way of showcasing patients and patient support organizations at the annual meeting. ASTRO uses this venue as an opportunity to raise awareness of the work these groups are doing, as well as raise money to help fund their support programs.

ASTRO also made a point of including other societies in its meetings. There were many innovations in 2005. For example ASTRO had a joint meeting with the Radiation Research Society (RRS) that year and there were luncheons and breakfasts with the American Association of Women Radiologists (AAWR).

In 2005 the National Cancer Institute (NCI) hosted a disparities session at ASTRO, a program spearheaded by the NCI designed to encourage minorities to enter into research trials as a way of improving the results of cancer treatment for these disadvantaged populations. In 2006, for the first time, several of the scientific sessions were translated into Spanish.

ASTRO President Nora Janjan opens the technical exhibits at the ASTRO annual meeting in New Orleans in 2002. Laura Thevenot, Mary Austin–Seymour, Colleen Lawton, and Dave Larson look on.

During the early years of the twenty-first century, ASTRO continued to grow and develop. As more patients received radiation therapy for the treatment of cancer, and healthcare costs continued to increase, ASTRO, with the enthusiastic participation of its physics members, became more involved with socioeconomic issues. Healthcare costs weren't increasing because more patients received radiation therapy; the cost of healthcare then was due, as it is now, to a multitude of factors, including new technologies, increased use of them and the cost of new medications. The society expanded its efforts in health policy and government relations and took a leadership

ASTRO President Joel Tepper awarding ASTRO's Gold Medal to Paul Wallner in 2003.

role in dealing with Medicare and Medicaid and with physician reimbursement for the ever-evolving technology of radiation oncology. In 2002, ASTRO was awarded full accreditation from the Accreditation Council for Continuing Medical Education (ACCME) to provide CME credits for its members.

The society also kept its members abreast of the new technology in radiation oncology. At the Phoenix annual meeting in 1998, ASTRO initiated a vascular radiotherapy roundtable to discuss the emerging technology of vascular brachytherapy. Earlier that year, ASTRO established a task force on vascular brachytherapy in order to make recommendations to the Board.[5]

K. Kian Ang awarding FASTRO certificate to Bahman Emami, first chair of the IMRT Practicum.

In the early twenty-first century, ASTRO initiated a yearly intensity modulated radiation therapy practicum to acquaint members with IMRT, the newest method of delivering treatments.

Small Meetings

Last but not least, ASTRO implemented a series of annual "small meetings" to supplement the society's scientific meeting in the fall of each year.

Beginning with a spring meeting in 1994, the small meetings format was designed to offer members the chance to catch up on continuing education in the fast-changing world of radiation oncology. David Larson recalled that some of them started when the ASTRO Board was trying to develop an ASTRO School of Radiation Oncology, similar to the School of Radiotherapy that the European Society of Therapeutic Radiology and Oncology (ESTRO) had begun a few years earlier to educate its members from the myriad of countries in Europe.[6]

David A. Larson, ASTRO president in 2000–2001.

The small meetings exposed ASTRO members to a veritable gamut of topics, starting in 1999. Biology meetings were held in 1999 and 2001 to focus on specific radiolobiological issues, and the 3-D/IMRT/IGRT (image guided radiotherapy) practicums have been conducted every year by a faculty of radiation oncologists and physicists since 2001 to teach members how to use the new conformal/IMRT technology. Outcomes research and quality assurance symposia were held in 2001, 2006, and 2007 to focus on delivering quality care to patients.

Translational research symposia were held in 2005, 2006, 2007, and 2008. Their purpose was to show how laboratory research can be translated into clinical studies or standard practice. ASTRO has also conducted symposia in conjunction with the ACR conference. The pre-ACR conference in 2000 dealt with integrating vascular brachytherapy into radiation oncology practice, and the topic in 2003 was molecular imaging.[7]

Since 2004, ASTRO has offered its members a host of small meetings that acquaint participants with particular treatment modalities and technological advancements. In 2004, as part of its pre-ACR symposium, ASTRO offered a session entitled "Brain Tumors: Evidence-based Decision Making in the New Millennium." That same year, the society sponsored radiation accident management courses and the popular STaRT (systemic targeted radionuclide therapy) program.[8]

ASTRO began its ongoing translational symposia in 2005 and began offering sessions in addition to its IMRT symposium. In 2006, ASTRO added sessions on IGRT, and the society's health services section sponsored the "Outcomes Research in Radiation Oncology Symposium" in September 2006. ASTRO also began sponsoring one-day sessions on quality assurance in 2007.[9]

Another outgrowth of the small meetings strategy implemented by ASTRO has been an invaluable tool for keeping members up to date on their certification. The ASTRO School of Radiation Oncology is for educating radiation oncologists. It started with the ancillary meetings, and according to Kathy Thomas of the ASTRO education staff, it has been extended into a distance-learning tool for radiation oncologists employing Web sites and other electronic media as part of the maintenance of certification (MOC) program of the American Board of Radiology.

The small meetings format and the School of Radiation Oncology are concrete ways in which ASTRO responded to the needs of its members in the twenty-first century. As ASTRO neared its fiftieth anniversary in 2008, the society was more relevant than ever—and ready to face new challenges at the dawn of its second half-century of service.

Self-Management

Steve Leibel remembered an ASTRO Board meeting at the American College of Radiology's Reston, Virginia, headquarters in 1997, the year he was the society's chairman. The ASTRO Board waited in a conference room of the building on Preston White Drive, only to discover that the staff assigned to ASTRO were attending another meeting off campus.

The Board was concerned. ASTRO had moved with ACR from Philadelphia to Reston two years before. "Our society was going through a lot of growing pains in the late 1990s," Leibel said.[10] Following that 1997 meeting, the ASTRO Board decided to prepare a strategic plan to consider the feasibility of self-management and separation from ACR.

"We had a session in my room," Leibel said. "One of our goals was for ASTRO to be a voice for radiation oncology, and we came out with our own strategic plan. But we didn't know how to handle government relations. Some of the senior folks in ASTRO thought that we should remain an educational organization. We did questionnaires on the subject and got past the opposition."[11]

Complicating the feelings among ASTRO Board members that ACR's management was stretched too thin was the perception that there was no day-to-day leadership of ASTRO operations. Nick Croce, the administrator who had overseen ASTRO's operations in the city of Philadelphia, left ASTRO in early 1998.

ASTRO had more than enough resources to go it alone. Leibel and Richard Hoppe were enabled in creating a self-managed society by the simple growth of ASTRO during the 1980s and 1990s. At the beginning of the 1980s, ASTRO's membership totaled 1,407. Total membership increased to 3,465 by 1990 and to 5,855 in 1998. Leibel's skillful presentation of a dues increase in 1996 and 1997 gave ASTRO the additional financial strength it needed to hire staff and lease property.[12]

Leibel and Hoppe recruited Frank Malouff from the American Podiatric Medical Association to serve as the first independent executive director of ASTRO. "It was clearly a defining moment for ASTRO," Leibel said.[13] ASTRO's move to self-management was followed almost immediately by a relocation of the offices to 12500 Fair Lakes Circle in Fairfax, Virginia, a fast-growing DC suburb. The Fairfax site was convenient to Dulles Airport and was a short taxicab ride from the nearest Metro station.

Frank Malouff, first full-time ASTRO executive director, 1997–2001.

"ACR has been extremely generous with ASTRO in sharing space and facilities," Malouff said at the time of the move. "However, ACR itself faces serious growth needs—and the building is only so large. So while we all are going to share a nostalgic moment on moving day, it is clearly necessary for both organizations that ASTRO gets its own home."[14]

Frank Malouff, a University of Colorado graduate with more than twenty years experience in healthcare and medical specialty society management, said his most challenging task involved "defining a new relationship with ACR. Everybody was feeling his way through it. John Curry, their executive director, was a guy in a very tough spot. The ACR really didn't want us to leave."[15]

Curry, the longtime executive director of ACR, said he felt that independence for the societies his office managed in Reston was almost a natural evolutionary phenomenon. "In Reston," Curry said, "we were managing the American Roentgen Ray Society (ARRS), the American Association of Women in Radiology (AAWR), and ASTRO. As each of these organizations gained financial security, they wanted more independence. ARRS, for example, bought its own building about the time that ASTRO moved into leased space on Fair Lakes Circle in Fairfax."[16]

Curry never looked at the 1998 separation of ASTRO and ACR as a parting of the ways. "There was never a split between the two organizations," he said. "There was always an inbred dependency on both sides. Neither wanted government relations run through the other."[17]

Malouff credited Frank Wilson with the quiet, behind-the-scenes negotiations that resulted in ASTRO leaving the ACR fold without burning bridges. "The hero of that saga is Frank Wilson," Malouff said. "He truly had everybody's best interest in mind. He was a very savvy political operator, both on an internal and external level."[18]

The Growth of Staff

In 1999, the year that ASTRO moved three miles south of the ACR general office building in Reston, the society's full-time staff had grown to seventeen. Just the year before, ASTRO's first as a self-managed society, Frank Malouff was ASTRO's only full-time employee; three staff members on loan from ACR were the only personnel to make the move down the street to the newly independent ASTRO office. Gregg Robinson, Kathy Thomas, Lucy Bedziak, and Keri Sperry were some of the earliest ASTRO staffers.

"Kathy, Gregg, and Lucy were the first three people loaned to us by ACR," Malouff said. "They were the core of the first staff in March 1998."[19] ASTRO quickly hired Cheryl Reinhardt as the society's corporate support staffer and Keri Sperry as a communications specialist. By May 1999, the ASTRO staff comprised seventeen people.[20]

David Hussey was an eyewitness to the changes that ASTRO experienced as a self-managed society in the early twenty-first century. From 1998 to 2001, he was part of an Executive Committee that included at various times Richard Hoppe, Larry Kun, Christopher Rose, Nora Janjan, and David Larson. Leibel and Hoppe had established the Executive Committee in 1997 when the society began to consider self-management. The Executive Committee was comprised of the ASTRO Board chair, the president, the president-elect, and later the immediate past-chair. It met weekly by conference call to discuss issues related to the society. Frank Mallouf, the executive director, also participated in those calls. The president-elect's job was to learn all he or she could about the Board of Directors. The president's responsibilities encompassed planning for the upcoming annual scientific meeting. The chairman, meanwhile, took care of the day-to-day operation of the society.

At the end of 2000, the Board of Directors decided that is was time to review how well the society was functioning. The first step of the process was an administrative evaluation by experts in society management. The Board solicited proposals from outside consultants. The Board spent weeks reviewing the eight proposals it received and eventually selected David Westman of McGladrey and Pullen to carry out the evaluation. Westman recruited Tom Nelson, a former executive director of the American Academy of Orthopaedic Surgeons, to assist him in the evaluation.[21]

Shortly after David Hussey stepped down as chair in late 2001, David Larson, the new incoming chairman, negotiated a severance agreement with Frank Malouff, who left ASTRO to pursue personal interests. David Westman, who had conducted the review, worked with the ASTRO Board to ensure a smooth transition. He offered the services of Tom Nelson, who agreed to take the executive director's position on an interim basis. "Tom Nelson did a wonderful job," Hussey explained. "He had a great personality, and he was an extremely effective administrator. Having been an executive director of a major medical organization, he was very knowledgeable about society administration."[22]

Even though the society went through a period of management upheaval, ASTRO was in excellent shape otherwise. In 2000, the society reported operating on a budget of $5 million, a figure that ASTRO leaders of just five years before would have found inconceivable. At the same time, registration at ASTRO's annual scientific meeting was rapidly increasing as well, approaching eight thousand that year.

Larson appointed a Search Committee headed by Joel Tepper to conduct a nation-wide search for Malouff's replacement. The committee's selection was Laura Thevenot, a fifteen-year veteran of healthcare organization management. Thevenot came to ASTRO in the summer of 2002 from her position as chief operating officer and executive vice president of the Federation of American Hospitals. Prior to that, Thevenot had been vice-president of federal affairs for the Health Insurance Association of America.[23]

Larson noted that Thevenot came to ASTRO with the reputation as "a consensus and coalition builder. She is highly regarded by healthcare, regulatory and government leaders."[24]

The Captains and Kings Depart

The old century didn't pass without a loss that truly marked the transition between the old ASTRO to the new ASTRO. On June 12, 1999, Juan del Regato, the last of the first three gold medalists, died at the age of ninety in Michigan. Del Regato had outlived Henry S. Kaplan, who died in 1984, and Gilbert Fletcher, who died in 1992. He also survived his wife of nearly sixty years, Inez, who died just months before her husband in the spring of 1999.[25]

Up until just months before his death, del Regato was a fascinating mix of the specialty's past and future. He was equally at ease regaling colleagues with stories of Marie Curie and Henri Coutard. In almost the next breath, del Regato was on the phone asking another colleague to help him in developing a Web site.[26]

Frank Wilson eulogized del Regato as "a determined and highly effective advocate for radiation oncology. Eloquent in three languages and a masterful diplomate, he was an extraordinarily charismatic and persuasive personality."[27]

A year before he died, del Regato sat with Keri Sperry, the managing editor of *ASTROnews*. When asked whether he considered himself a physican, researcher or a scientist, del Regato was emphatic in his

Theodore Lawrence, ASTRO president in 2003–2004, recognizes Prabhakar Tripuraneni, his successor in 2004–2005.

Top: Joel E. Tepper, ASTRO president in 2002–2003.

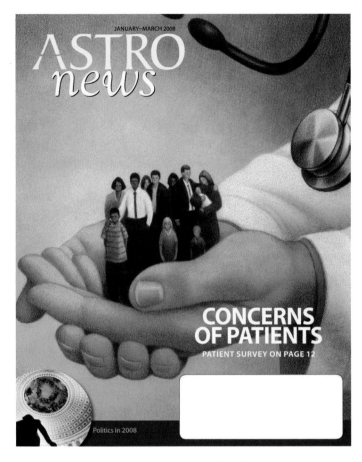

JANUARY–MARCH 2008

ASTRO
news

CONCERNS
OF PATIENTS
PATIENT SURVEY ON PAGE 12

Politics in 2008

ASTROnews, *a magazine delivered to ASTRO members to keep them informed of issues related to radiation oncology, has been in continuous circulation since the late 1990s.*

response. "I see myself as a physician," he said. "Therapeutic radiology is basically a clinical experience. Believing that radiation therapy was a technical thing was an error that was committed by many. You need to be a clinician in this specialty. That's why it is difficult to train radiotherapists."[28]

Creating the Foundation

For many years, ASTRO had run an Education and Development Foundation that existed primarily to fund research awards in radiation oncology. The E&D Fund was mostly a pass through though, with the money to fund the awards largely coming from ASTRO each year to pay for the awards.

In 2000–2001, David Larson and his chair, David Hussey, wanted to change the fund to become more of an active foundation that raised money from individuals and corporations and was a more self-sufficient organization. "In this way," Hussey said, "it would help provide funding for those ASTRO volunteers who do the research, present the papers, and offer the refresher courses at our meetings. The foundation should make it easier for them to do their job and reward them in a small way for what they do and have done for the Society."

Sarah Donaldson was appointed chair of a committee to explore establishing a foundation, but the economic conditions in 2001 were not favorable. Wall Street was unstable at the time when the technology boom that had driven the financial markets through much of the 1990s collapsed. The foundation idea was then put on hold until 2007 when ASTRO's Board voted to launch the Radiation Oncology Institute.

A Commitment to Reorganization and Strategic Planning

Education and research, long a dual mission of ASTRO, was codified in the society's governance structure following the completion of the strategic plan in 2002. In early 2001, the ASTRO Board authorized the Executive Committee to set in motion a new strategic plan, the fourth since the late 1980s. Larry Kun was appointed to head the first Strategic Planning Committee.[29]

Kun and his committee worked throughout 2001 and delivered their report to the Executive Committee in the summer of 2002 and to the membership at the business meeting held in conjunction with the annual meeting in the fall of 2002. It was, as Larson described the strategic plan, "an in depth look at the governance structures and processes of ASTRO.

How we can increase our efficiency and effectiveness as an organization was foremost in our discussions."[30]

The 2001 strategic plan, which was presented to the membership in late 2002, involved an enormous amount of time and effort on the part of both ASTRO's board and staff.

The plan resulted in the establishment of a large number of very concrete goals, including the important notion that the society would strive to be more proactive than reactive. The plan also helped move the society to a better understanding of the role it should play in the development of healthcare economics, government regulations, education and research.

The 2001 plan's change in focus led inevitably to a major change in the way in which ASTRO governed itself. "The proposed changes dictate that, rather than rely on a loose web of committees, ASTRO's committees should be reorganized into four main Councils—Education, Healthcare Economics, Government Relations and Research," Larson explained to the membership. "These are the areas in which our members consistently request action by ASTRO."[31]

Leonard L. Gunderson, ASTRO Treasurer/Secretary.

Each of the four proposed councils would have a very specific mission and would be governed by a chair and a vice-chair. The job of the council leaders, who would be assisted by assigned staff, would be to identify future trends and challenges to the specialty, oversee and steer the activities of the committees within their council and report back to the Board of Directors on actions taken by their council. The council structure was designed to ensure that important work would be completed in an efficient and timely manner.[32]

"When it comes time for you to vote on these governance changes," Larson said, "I hope you will keep in mind that they will position ASTRO to strengthen and increase our activities in the four key areas."[33] The membership did approve the governance changes in 2003, and this governance structure has been in place since then. In 2001, the membership initially rejected a request for a second dues increase in seven years. Later in 2002, members approved a small dues increase by a 69 percent margin.[34]

The importance ascribed to government relations and health policy issues by the membership was perhaps the central element of the new governance structure. Underscoring that importance was the financial support that ASTRO's Board provided to these functions in the new century. Between 1998 and 2002, ASTRO increased its annual expenditures for government relations and economics from $96,590 to $673,850.[35]

Nora Janjan, who succeeded Larson as chair for 2002–2003, was a member of the Strategic Planning Committee. "Speaking as both a member of the Board of Directors and the Strategic Planning Committee," Janjan said, "I can say that all of us who participated in the strategic planning truly believe that these changes are necessary for the future strength of our Society and our specialty."[36]

Endnotes

1. David Hussey Comments to the Author, February 24, 2008.

2. David Hussey e-mail to the author, January 4, 2008, p. 1.

3. Ibid.

4. David Hussey Comments to the Author, February 24, 2008.

5. Phoenix, *ASTRO News,* November/December 1998, p. 4.

6. David Larson Comment to the Author, February 20, 2008.

7. *ASTRO School of Radiation Oncology—Small Meetings, 1994 through 2008.*

8. Ibid.

9. Ibid.

10. Interview with Steven Leibel, p. 2.

11. Ibid., p. 3.

12. "American Society for Therapeutic Radiology and Oncology-Vital Statistics," *ASTROnews,* July/August 1998, p. 2.

13. Interview with Steven Leibel, p. 3.

14. Frank Malouff, "Executive Insights," *ASTROnews,* May/June 1999, p. 3.

15. Digitally Recorded Telephone Oral History Interview with Frank Malouff, Fairfax, Virginia, March 4, 2008, p. 3.

16. Interview with John Curry, p. 4.

17. Ibid.

18. Digitally Recorded Telephone Oral History Interview with Frank Malouff, Fairfax, Virginia, March 4, 2008, p. 3.

19. Ibid., p. 4.

20. Ibid.

21. Interview with John Curry, p. 1.

22. Tape-recorded Telephone Oral History Interview with David Hussey, San Antonio, Texas, January 2, 2008, p. 3.

23. "Board of Directors Names New Executive Director," *ASTROnews,* July–September 2002, p. 6.

24. David Larson, "Chairman's Update—Making a Difference," *ASTROnews,* July–September 2002, p. 4.

25. "Juan del Regato," *ASTROnews,* July/August 1999, p. 5.

26. "In Tribute to Dr. del Regato" by Larry E. Kuhn, MD, FACR, *ASTROnews,* July/August 1999, p. 5.

27. "In Tribute to Dr. del Regato" by J. Frank Wilson, MD, FACR, *ASTROnews,* July/August 1999, p. 5.

28. Keri Sperry, "Personal Impact: Excerpts from a Conversation with the late Dr. Juan del Regato," *ASTROnews,* January/February 2000, p. 5.

39. Tape-recorded Telephone Oral History Interview with David Hussey, San Antonio, Texas, January 2, 2008, p. 3.

30. David Larson, "Chairman's Update," *ASTROnews,* January–March 2002, p. 6.

31. David Larson, "Chairman's Update—Making a Difference," *ASTROnews,* July–September 2002, p. 4.

32. Ibid., p. 5.

33. Ibid.

34. Nora Janjan, "Chairman's Update," *ASTROnews,* January–March 2003, p. 4.

35. David Larson, "Chairman's Update," *ASTROnews,* January–March 2002, p. 4.

36. Nora Janjan, "Chairman's Update," *ASTROnews,* October–December 2002, p. 5.

Annual meeting attendees enthusiastically embraced eLearning sessions, requiring expansion of the number of sessions and number of computer stations, such as at this 2007 session.

CHAPTER TWELVE

ASTRO Today and Tomorrow

ASTRO looks back on fifty years of history with a confidence born of experience and an optimism about the society's ability to meet the challenges of the next half-century. It is the largest radiation oncology society in the world with nearly ten thousand members from a variety of fields related to the treatment of cancer with radiation. The membership includes radiation oncologists, physicians in related fields, medical physicists, radiobiologists and other scientists interested in cancer and the treatment of cancer with radiation, radiation therapists, oncology nurses, radiation oncology administrators, and radiation oncology residents.

As has been the case since the beginning of the society in 1958, ASTRO's membership is comprised of healthcare professionals from community and academic medical centers across the United States, as well as professionals from a score of foreign countries.[1]

ASTRO is the premier professional society for radiation oncology today. It is dedicated to improving patient care through education, the advancement of science, and representation in the health policy arena. Its mission is to advance the practice of radiation oncology by promoting excellence in patient care, by providing opportunities for educational development, promoting research and disseminating research results, and by representing radiation oncology in a rapidly evolving healthcare environment. It has truly become the "Voice of Radiation Oncology" in the United States.

Public and Patient Education

Within the medical community itself, ASTRO has become an advocate for a team approach to treating cancer, fostering a cooperative effort among radiation oncologists, medical oncologists, surgeons, and other physicians.

ASTRO continues to publish educational materials for the public aimed at keeping patients informed about the role of radiation therapy. It works with the media to promote accurate articles on scientific breakthroughs involving radiation therapies and takes a major role in the development of legislation and regulations affecting patient care.[2]

For nearly five years, ASTRO has focused on educating people on the benefits of radiation oncology as a treatment modality in the quest to control cancer. "One of our key initiatives is the building of our public awareness campaign," said Laura Thevenot, the society's chief executive officer.[3]

ASTRO started to produce brochures to explain to patients their treatment options. To date, the society has produced fifteen patient education brochures and has distributed more than six hundred thousand of the publications. Three of the brochures have been translated into Spanish; nine have been translated into Arabic. As a result, the brochures have won national and international awards in recent years.

"We work very closely with the patient advocacy groups," Thevenot said. "We often have them review the brochures before we print them, so they can assist us with ensuring the content includes answers to the questions patients have. We also convened focus groups to see what kind of language resonates with the public."[4]

Another major step forward in public education has involved the society's creation of a comprehensive patient Web site. The URL for the new Web site is www.rtanswer.org. Thevenot explained that *RT Answers* allows patients to access the latest information about radiation therapy treatments.[5]

ASTRO completely redesigned its Web site in 2007 to better communicate with its members. The new site includes a more comprehensive meetings section; a new education portal—ASTRO School of Radiation Oncology (ASRO); an updated job placement center; and an expanded press room that contains all the latest information on the society and its programs,

Omar Salazar's voice helped forge positive relations between ASTRO and radiation oncologists and professional medical societies in Latin America and Spain.

Patricia J. Eifel, president in 2007–2008.

ASTRO held its first eLearning sessions at the annual meeting in 2001, and the concept was well entrenched when this session took place in 2006.

including downloadable photos for the media, contacts for radiation therapy experts. and up-to-the-minute news on ASTRO.[6]

The year before the Web redesign, ASTRO created a Web template that offered the patient education content available on the *RT Answers* Web site to its members. About 150 ASTRO members have taken advantage of the free service, and more ASTRO members have adapted content from the *RT Answers* for their practice's Web sites. Thevenot said "It is a good way to get information into patients' hands. And that is a growing priority for the Society."[7]

The War Against Cancer

ASTRO's more than nine thousand members are foot soldiers in one of the more important battles the American medical community is waging in the twenty-first century. In 2008, more than 1.4 million new cases of cancer will have been diagnosed in the United States, and some five hundred thousand Americans will die of the disease during the year. The leading cause of death among Americans over the age of eighty-five, and the second leading cause of death among all Americans, cancer annually accounts for one in four US deaths.[8]

In 2004, the year with the latest comprehensive statistics, nearly one million patients in the United States were treated with radiation therapy, the vast majority of them by ASTRO members. Those 1 million patients made about 23.4 million radiation therapy treatment visits to 2,010 hospitals and freestanding radiation therapy centers. About 60 percent of the patients treated in 2004 had not previously received radiation therapy.[9] Radiotherapy plays a growing role in organ-sparing cancer management.

With baby boomers quickly reaching the fifth and sixth decade of life, the fight that ASTRO has been waging against cancer becomes even more critical than it has been in the past. More than three-quarters of all cancers

The current ASTRO Logo.

ASTRO started the Survivor Circle to recognize cancer support organizations in the annual meeting host city.

FASTRO

In 2006, ASTRO introduced its ASTRO Fellows program, which was quickly dubbed FASTRO. Eligibility is based upon length of membership, as well as meritorious service to the society and to the field of radiation oncology. Members can follow any of four pathways to becoming a Fellow, including leadership/service, research, patient care, or education. The length of membership criteria is twenty years, but plans call for that requirement to be lowered to ten years in the future. The first group of ASTRO Fellows was inducted during the 2006 annual meeting in Philadelphia. The FASTRO program was created in 2006 by Prabhakar Tripuraneni.

The first ASTRO Fellows class in 2006.

Top: ASTRO President K. Kian Ang, FASTRO, inducts Nancy Ellerbroek as a 2007 Fellow.

Middle, left: Barbara Fowble is inducted as an ASTRO Fellow by ASTRO President K. Kian Ang at the annual meeting in Los Angeles in 2007.

Middle, right: ASTRO Fellowship Certificate awarded to Prabhakar Tripuraneni in November 2006, and signed by members of the ASTRO Board for his work in developing the ASTRO Fellowship Program during his term of ASTRO leadership in 2004-2005.

ASTRO's past year's accomplishments and future plans are summarized and reported on, while outgoing officers are thanked and incoming officers are introduced.

Top: ASTRO President K. Kian Ang addressing a plenary session at the society's annual meeting.

are diagnosed in patients fifty-five and older. Men are particularly susceptible to prostate, lung, and colorectal cancer, while women typically fall prey to breast, lung, and colorectal cancer.[10] Lung cancer remains the top cancer killer for both men and women. For these types of cancer, radiotherapy plays a very significant role in their management. Other cancers continue to be a significant cause of death, even among the young. Leukemia is the most common cancer among those younger than fourteen.[11]

ASTRO makes contributions in the war against cancer through its ability to make possible cutting-edge research. The annual meetings and subsidiary meetings place high priority on critical presentations of research findings from the laboratory (physics and biology) as well as the clinic. "The society is not doing research, per se," said Thevenot, "but we are facilitating research through grant programs. Currently, ASTRO provides nearly $1 million annually to fund research."[12]

Foundation Dreams and Strategic Plans

As part of its fiftieth anniversary celebration, ASTRO is in the planning stages of launching a foundation to fund the research, education, and public outreach activities that have become such a critical part of the society's mission. "We've created the Radiation Oncology Institute, or ROI, to help us with this effort," Thevenot said. "We've got commitments for $5 million so far. The goal is to create a long-term endowment within the foundation that can be used to fund programs that are important to radiation oncology."[13] The Radiation Oncology Institute is scheduled to be officially unveiled to the membership in 2009.

Another initiative that is on the horizon is a new strategic plan. "This past year," Thevenot said, "we brought in outside consultants to help us redo the strategic plan totally. Leadership felt that it would be better for the Society to take a fresh look at the plan and not be driven by the old language. The Board felt it would be a useful exercise for people to look at it with a new set of eyes."[14]

Thevenot noted that ASTRO proactively updates its strategic plan periodically. Those updates always proceed with the goals that ten years in the future ASTRO will continue to be the premier society for radiation oncologists, that ASTRO will provide outstanding educational opportunities

Members throng the exhibit hall during each year's annual meeting.

for its members, and that ASTRO will support and advocate scientific research. Finally, the updates of the strategic plan mandate that ASTRO promote broader community understanding of the specialty of radiation oncology through its publications, advocacy efforts and by the example of its members.[15]

Advocacy: A New and Important Role for ASTRO

What an earlier generation of ASTRO leadership called socioeconomic issues today's leaders define as the society's health policy and government relations functions. "It has taken us six years to build those functions," Thevenot said.

In 2002, when Thevenot arrived at ASTRO, the society did legislative monitoring. "It was not full-blown advocacy as yet," she said. "Our advocates all had day jobs. We've always relied heavily on our volunteers for advocacy."[16] In the past, ASTRO was trying to influence governmental officials with volunteers and part-time staff, but it was becoming increasingly clear that the organization had to develop a full-time cadre of professional governmental relations experts to accomplish meaningful results.

ASTRO's leadership gave the green light to Thevenot to put a staff together to address health policy and government relations functions in 2003. By 2004, the society had assembled a staff of five people in health policy and four in government relations.

For much of its history, ASTRO had delegated the responsibility for dealing with socioeconomic issues to the American College of Radiology (ACR). One of the goals the Board set when it hired Thevenot was to bring ASTRO to the next level when it came to dealing with health policy and government relations.

"When I came to ASTRO," Thevenot said, "we had split off from ACR but were still tied to them through our Joint Economic and Government Relations Committees. And we certainly didn't have our own health policy

Laura Thevenot has been ASTRO executive director since 2002.

George Laramore, chair of the Government Relations Council.

Albert Blumberg, chair of the Government Relations Council.

expertise in-house. It is a somewhat complex area, and ACR had a lot of other things on its plate."[17]

Thevenot noted that ACR deserves a lot of credit for helping ASTRO move forward with its health policy and government relations initiatives. ACR and ASTRO realized that it benefited both organizations to work together closely and collaboratively with each other. "They definitely helped us build our advocacy," she said.[18]

Still, as late as 2004, if congressional staffers or government agency personnel had a question about radiation therapy, they were as likely to call ACR as they were to call ASTRO. But by 2004, ASTRO had developed in-house expertise to deal with complex health policy issues, such as imaging regulations in the balanced budget legislation and securing appropriate codes. "Our government relations staff is working with other cancer organizations to educate Congress about the importance of cancer research funding," Thevenot said.[19]

One thing that ASTRO's government relations staff targeted was the importance of educating lawmakers and agency staff about radiation oncology and what it accomplishes. "This is the fifth year of ASTRO sponsoring its government relations Advocacy Day," Thevenot said. "The first year, 6 ASTRO members said they might come, and we decided to cancel the whole event. The second year, we had maybe 25 people, and the third year about 50 going to the Hill and various government agencies. Now, we are up to 110 people at the event."[20]

Thevenot pointed out that "going to the Hill has been an education process for our membership. In the past, it was always, 'Oh, you're a radiologist.' For us, it was a process of defining what a radiation oncologist is. It does take awhile to build recognition, but now, people on the Hill call us about issues. We have made great strides in being the voice of radiation oncology. The people in Congress and at the FDA and NIH all know who we are."[21]

Health Policy and Government Relations

Like it has been almost since the start, ASTRO is a society that depends on its members for input and action. Never big enough to afford a massive staff, ASTRO has always asked its members to volunteer their expertise and time.

The Health Policy Council is typical of the volunteer nature of ASTRO. The Council consists of five subcommittees that examine a wide variety of issues important to society members. The Health Policy Committee, consisting of the chairs and vice-chairs of all the Health Policy Subcommittees, reports directly to the Health Policy Council chair and vice-chair on the status of tasks undertaken and completed by the other Health Policy committees. Those committees include the Code Development and Valuation Committee, the Code Utilization and Application Committee, the Emerging Technology Committee, the Payment Systems Committee, and the Regulatory Committee.[22]

The Government Relations staff works together with the Health Policy staff to further the interests of society members and the patients they serve. The Government Relations staff raises funds for ASTRO PAC, the Political Action Committee the Board established in 2003, and it represents the society before the US Congress, the White House, and other federal agencies and entities.[23]

"For the first time this past year," Thevenot noted, "there was legislation moving forward in the Congress in which our Government Relations staff got language inserted that delineated the difference between radiation oncology and diagnostic radiology. They are different, and they should be treated differently in the legislation. This was an important victory for ASTRO and radiation oncology."[24]

The Voice of Radiation Oncology

As ASTRO begins its second half-century of existence, the society truly has become the voice of radiation oncology. Representing a practice that was essentially in its infancy fifty years ago and has matured into a respected component of the cancer team, the society's growth has paralleled that of the specialty. A society that never employed more than three or four full-time staff members until ten years ago now has a staff of fifty-two people, most of them specialists in specific areas, such as education, event planning, health policy, public relations, research, and government affairs.

As ASTRO progresses into its sixth decade and beyond, the scope of its programs will continuously expand with the fantastic rate of advances in science in biology and physics. The interest of ASTRO's members and the content of national meetings and educational programs will be based on increasing interactions with physicists, physiologists [organism, tissue and cellular], and geneticists. The physicists are expected to develop the technologies for 4-D image guided external beam radiation therapy and the resultant steadily decreasing PTVs (planning target volumes), image guided brachytherapy, and the expansion of the array of available radiation beams.

In parallel there is the expectation that the genetic characterization of the tumor and normal tissues will help create a design management strategy for the best feasible outcome for each patient. These technical and biological gains will, no doubt, yield increasing proportions of patients free of tumor in the irradiated volume and free of treatment-related morbidity. This intimate collaboration between scientists and physicians will modify ASTRO's educational programs as well as the format and con-

Louis Harrison, ASTRO president in 2006–2007, and Bruce Minsky, chair of the Education Council.

Anthony Zeitman, chair of the Education Council.

tent of its national meetings. In its fiftieth year, the ASTRO and Radiation Research Society meetings are held at the same time and the same site with some combined sessions. This has occurred once previously, and ASTRO's commingling with biologists and physicists is sure to become more frequent and intense in the years ahead, with the ultimate benefit accruing to ASTRO's patients.

The society will undoubtedly face challenges in the years to come. But no matter the challenges, ASTRO will continue to serve as the Voice of Radiation Oncology. It will continue to be an effective advocate for the radiation therapy community. It also will encourage an unwavering support for education and research since those goals have been the main missions of the society since it was founded in 1958.

The founders would no doubt approve.

Endnotes

1. *About the American Society for Therapeutic Radiology and Oncology*, ASTRO Fact Sheet, n.d.

2. Ibid.

3. Digitally Recorded Telephone Oral History Interview with Laura Thevenot, Fairfax, Virginia, p. 6.

4. Ibid., p. 7.

5. Ibid.

6. *ASTRO Redesigns, Launches New Web Site*, ASTRO Press Release, February 15, 2007.

7. Digitally Recorded Telephone Oral History Interview with Laura Thevenot, Fairfax, Virginia, p. 7.

8. *ASTRO, Fast Facts About Cancer*, 2007.

9. *ASTRO, Fast Facts About Radiation Therapy*.

10. Ibid.

11. Ibid.

12. Digitally Recorded Telephone Oral History Interview with Laura Thevenot, Fairfax, Virginia, p. 8.

13. Ibid.

14. Ibid.

15. *ASTRO's Strategic Plan*, www.ASTRO.org.

16. Ibid., p. 2.

17. Ibid., p. 1.

18. Ibid., pp. 1–2.

19. Ibid., p. 2.

20. Ibid., p. 3.

21. Ibid.

22. *ASTRO's Health Policy Council Consists of Six Committees*, www.ASTRO.org.

23. *Government Relations*, www.ASTRO.org.

24. Digitally Recorded Telephone Oral History Interview with Laura Thevenot, Fairfax, Virginia, p. 6.

APPENDICES

2006 Fellows Class

Sucha O. Asbell, MD
Mary M. Austin-Seymour, MD
Malcolm A. Bagshaw, MD
David C. Beyer, MD
Carl R. Bogardus Jr., MD
Luther W. Brady, MD
Theodore J. Brickner Jr., MD
G. Stephen Brown, MD
J. Martin Brown, PhD
Komanduri K. N. Charyulu, MD
George T. Y. Chen, PhD
Lawrence R. Coia, MD
C. Norman Coleman, MD
Jay S. Cooper, MD
James D. Cox, MD
Giulio J. D'Angio, MD
Lawrence W. Davis, MD
Luis Delclos, MD, DMSc
William C. Dewey, PhD
Sarah S. Donaldson, MD
Robert W. Edland, MD
Benedick A. Fraass, PhD
Zvi Y. Fuks, MD
Dale E. Fuller, MD
James M. Galvin, DSc
Eli J. Glatstein, MD
Michael Goitein, PhD

Eric J. Hall, DSc
Gerald E. Hanks, MD
Jay R. Harris, MD
Samuel Hellman, MD
Frank R. Hendrickson, MD
Richard T. Hoppe, MD
Peter R. Hulick, MS, MD
David H. Hussey, MD
Nora Janjan, MD
Karen King-Wah Fu, MD
Ritsuko U. Komaki, MD
Larry E. Kun, MD
David A. Larson, MD, PhD
Theodore S. Lawrence, MD, PhD
Steven A. Leibel, MD
Seymour H. Levitt, MD, DSc
Allen S. Lichter, MD
Victor A. Marcial, MD
Luka Milas, MD, PhD
Rodney R. Million, MD
Bharat B. Mittal, MD
Eleanor D. Montague, MD
William T. Moss, MD
Stanley E. Order, MD
Carlos A. Perez, MD
Lester J. Peters, MD
Theodore L. Phillips, MD
Leonard R. Prosnitz, MD
James A. Purdy, PhD
Christopher M. Rose, MD

Marvin Rotman, MD
Philip Rubin, MD
Charles W. Scarantino, MD, PhD
Robert J. Shalek, PhD, JD
William U. Shipley, MD
Michael L. Steinberg, MD
Herman D. Suit, MD, DPhil
Nagalingham Suntharalingam, PhD
Randall K. Ten Haken, PhD
Joel E. Tepper, MD
Howard Thames, PhD
John W. Travis, MD, DSc
Prabhakar Tripuraneni, MD
Lynn J. Verhey, PhD
Paul Wallner, DO
J. Frank Wilson, MD, FACR
H. Rodney Withers, MD, DSc
Harvey B. Wolkov, MD, FACR

2007 Fellows Class

K. Kian Ang, MD, PhD
James A. Belli, MD
Arthur L. Boyer, MD
James R. Cassady, MD
Bernard J. Cummings, MB, ChB
D. Jeffery Demanes, MD

R. L. Scotte Doggett, MD
John D. Earle, MD
Patricia J. Eifel, MD
Nancy A. Ellerbroek, MD
Bahman Emami, MD
Barbara L. Fowble, MD
Mary K. Gospodarowicz, MD
Leonard L. Gunderson, MD
Dennis E. Hallahan, MD
Kenneth R. Hogstrom, PhD
Geoffrey S. Ibbott, PhD
Madhu John, MD
Herbert D. Kerman, MD
Henry M. Keys, MD
Deborah A. Kuban, MD
George E. Laramore, MD
Colleen F. Lawton, MD
C. Clifton Ling, PhD
Carl M. Mansfield, MD, ScD
Peter M. Mauch, MD
Beryl McCormick, MD
Ruby F. Meredith, MD, PhD
Gustavo S. Montana, MD
Ravinder Nath, PhD
Brian O'Sullivan, MD
Colin A. Poulter, MD
Timothy E. Schultheiss, PhD
James G. Schwade, MD
Patrick R. M. Thomas, MB, BS
Elizabeth L. Travis, PhD

Raul C. Urtasun, MD
Mahesh K. Varia, MD
William M. Wara, MD
Todd H. Wasserman, MD
Moody Wharam Jr., MD

2008 Fellows Class

John M. Bedwinek, MD
Chu Huai Chang, MD
Donald S. Childs Jr., MD
Florence H. C. Chu, MD
Joseph P. Concannon, MD
Louis S. Constine, MD
Laurie E. Gaspar, MD, MBA
Shankar P. Giri, MD
Ruth J. Guttmann, MD
Bruce G. Haffty, MD
Louis B. Harrison, MD
Joseph S. Kong, MD
Mary K. Martel, PhD
John L. Meyer, MD
Lowell S. Miller, MD
Donn G. Mosser, MD
Walter T. Murphy, MD
Dattatreyudu Nori, MD
James R. Oleson, MD, PhD
Ajmel A. Puthawala, MD

Abram Recht, MD
Robert Robbins, MD
Robert H. Sagerman, MD
Paul W. Scanlon, MD
Brenda Shank, MD, PhD
Edward G. Shaw, MD
Lawrence J. Solin, MD
Orliss Wildermuth, MD
Albert L. Wiley Jr., MD, PhD
Steven R. Zeidner, MD

ASTRO
Gold Medalists:

1977 Juan del Regato
     Gilbert H. Fletcher
     Henry S. Kaplan
1978 Franz J. Buschke
     Edith H. Quimby
1979 Isadore Lampe
     M. Vera Peters
1980 Harold E. Johns
     Simon Kramer
1981 William T. Moss
1982 Morton M. Kligerman
1983 Mortimer M. Elkind
1984 Philip Rubin
1985 Malcolm A. Bagshaw
1986 Walter D. Rider
1987 Luther W. Brady
1988 William E. Powers
1989 Robert G. Parker
1990 Samuel Hellman
     Herman D. Suit
1991 H. Rodney Withers
     Seymour H. Levitt
1992 Eleanor D. Montague
     Carlos A. Perez
1993 Eric J. Hall
     John S. Laughlin
     Theodore Phillips
1994 James D. Cox
     Gerald E. Hanks
1995 John F. Fowler
     Rodney R. Million

1996 Zvi Y. Fuks
     Robert J. Shalek
1997 Luis Delclos
     Chiu-Chen Wang
1998 Theodore J. Brickner Jr.
     William C. Dewey
1999 J. Martin Brown
     Giulio J. D'Angio
2000 Sarah S. Donaldson
     James A. Purdy
2001 Karen King-Wah Fu
     Howard Thames
2002 Steven A. Leibel
     Victor A. Marcial
     Marvin Rotman
2003 Michael Goitein
     Lester J. Peters
     J. Frank Wilson
2004 Eli J. Glatstein
     Luka Milas
     Paul Wallner
2005 C. Norman Coleman
     Allen S. Lichter
2006 Richard T. Hoppe
     C. Clifton Ling
2007 Jay R. Harris
     Larry Kun
2008 Christopher M. Rose
     Joel Tepper

ASTRO
Honorary Members:

1989 Frank Ellis
     Saul A. Rosenberg
     Norman M. Bleehen
1990 Harold B. Hewitt
1991 Nicholas Cassisi
1992 Roanld A. Castellino
1993 Gerald Marks
1994 Helmuth Goepfert
     David P. Winchester
1995 David Bragg
1996 William C. Wood
1997
1998 John H. Glick
     Frances Glica
1999 James M. Moorefield
2000 Bernard Fisher
2001 Richard Klausner
2002 Ann Barrett
     John J. Curry
2003 Frederick Eilber
     LaSalle D. Laffall Jr.
2004 Umberto Veronisi
2005 Francis J. Mahoney
2006 William Thorwarth Jr.
2007 Randal S. Weber
2008 Audrey Evans

INDEX